BUILD YOUR BEST WRITING LIFE

ESSENTIAL STRATEGIES FOR PERSONAL WRITING SUCCESS

KRISTEN KIEFFER

Build Your Best Writing Life: Essential Strategies for Personal Writing Success

First Edition (2019).

The advice contained within this book is based on my personal experience as an author. I am not a publishing industry professional, psychologist, lawyer, or career coach. Please apply the advice contained herein to your writing life at your own discretion.

ISBN: 978-1-7342064-0-1

Published by She's Novel Press.

Cover design by Jelena Mirkovic Jankovic.

Editing by Sara Letourneau and Sarah Kolb-Williams.

Printed in the United States of America.

❀ Created with Vellum

CONTENTS

Introduction   v

PART I
THE CREATIVE MINDSET

1. The Root of Creative Frustration   3
2. Cultivating Confidence in Your Writing   11
3. Owning Your Originality   19
4. The Only Way to Do the Damn Hard Work   27

PART II
THE WRITING PRACTICE

5. Inspiration, Motivation, and the Power of   37
   Creative Habit
6. Building a Sustainable Writing Practice   43
7. The Key to Making Time to Write   49
8. Claiming Your Creative Workspace   55
9. Rocking Your Writing Process   63
10. Improving Your Writing Output   73
11. Refilling the Creative Well   79
12. Working Through Writer's Block   85
13. Building Writing Endurance   91

PART III
TOOLS FOR INTENTIONAL GROWTH

14. The Power in Seeking Intentional Growth   101
15. Studying the Craft   113
16. Consuming Critically   121
17. Seeking Constructive Feedback   129
18. Accessing Your Full Imagination   137

PART IV
THE ROAD TO WRITING SUCCESS

19. Who Are You as a Writer?   147
20. What Does Writing Success Mean to You?   153
21. Crafting a Writer's Mission Statement   159

22. Choosing the Publishing Path That's Right for You   165

23. Business Models for Authors   173

24. Growing an Avid Readership   181

25. Creating Your Writing Road Map   189

   –Writing Roadmap Example 1   196

   –Writing Roadmap Example 2   197

   –Writing Roadmap Example 3   198

Conclusion   199

AFTER READING

Author's Note   205

Acknowledgments   207

Creative Affirmations   209

Bibliography   211

Endnotes   214

About the Author   215

INTRODUCTION

BECOMING THE WRITER YOU WANT TO BE

Five years ago, I was tired.

Tired of staring at my computer folder full of unfinished manuscripts. Tired of rewriting the same opening chapters for a story I'd been working on for years. Tired of feeling like I'd never become the writer I wanted to be. I had big dreams for my writing life, but those dreams seemed light-years away, and I didn't know how to make them a reality. I yearned for the early days of my writing life, when spending time with my characters was a cherished joy rather than the chore it had become.

When exactly had this fatigue set in? When had I started to fear and even loathe the blank page? As it turned out, I could pinpoint that catalyst, the very moment I began to find writing daunting and draining. It happened when I first considered that perhaps my big writing dreams didn't have to remain dreams. Perhaps I could take steps to turn them into realities: to land an agent, land a book deal, publish novel after novel, and become a best-selling success.

When I began to treat these dreams as serious possibilities, fear set in. I tried to research my way out of this fear, to learn everything I could about what it would take to make my writing dreams a reality. But the more I learned, the deeper fear sank its teeth into me. It was as though it pierced the skin of some protective membrane around my hope, my confidence, my joy. "You can't possibly become an author," fear said. "Look how much work your story needs to be as good as the stories you love. You don't have the talent to write books like that. Agents and publishers will laugh in your face."

I tried to fight against fear, but sitting down to write felt more and more demoralizing with every passing day. I couldn't see beyond all the ways in which my story failed to measure up. My characters were bland and uninteresting, mere shadows of the ones I loved from other books. The few interesting scenes I had written were disjointed. They lacked structure, purpose, and a compelling narrative thread. And my prose? Lord, my prose. I had no idea how to lay down a sentence I didn't immediately want to ink with red. Still, I kept striving.

This push and pull between fear and hope, between defeat and stubborn determination, persisted day after day, week after week, until at last, after years of mounting frustration, I found myself faced with a choice: I could give up writing for good, or I could figure out, once and for all, how to build the writing life I wanted to lead.

Five years later, I'm grateful I chose the path of hope.

Are you willing to do the same?

If so, this book will serve as your road map to becoming the writer you long to be. The principles in this book are applicable to you no matter your definition of writing success. Whether you want to top best-seller lists, build a thriving career as an indie author, write popular online fan fiction, or finally finish that story you've been meaning to share with family and friends, this book will help you achieve your goals for your writing life by teaching you how to do what unsuccessful writers don't do: put in the work.

Building your best writing life isn't easy. But if you commit to putting in the time and effort necessary to become the writer you want to be, you will become that writer. It's as simple as that. Yet the writerly struggle to sit down and do creative work is all too common. So common, in fact, that it's even become the butt of online jokes and memes: "A day may come when I conquer procrastination and write the second page of this novel, but it is not this day!"

But why not this day? What makes writing so difficult when it's what writers so desperately want to do?

The answer to this question is rooted in fear, and fear is tricky. It manifests itself in so many shapes and sizes, in complaints and excuses and doubts and false beliefs, that I like to call fear by a different name: resistance. It's the creative's mortal enemy. The obstacle in your path to writing success. Resistance takes one look at the road to your best writing life, finds that it isn't paved with gold, and sets out to deter and distract you at every turn. If you're frustrated with the writing life you're leading, you've likely allowed resistance to succeed.

Without adopting strong strategies for dealing with resistance, you won't become the writer you want to be. That is why part 1 of this book tackles the creative mindset, arming you with the strategies you need to cultivate confidence in your skills and stories—and, more importantly, in your ability to do the damn hard work.

With that confidence in place, part 2 of this book will guide you in developing a writing practice that doesn't wreak havoc on your creative energies, one that sees you putting in the work using methods and techniques best suited to your schedule, preferences, and personal creative process. But even consistently putting your fingers on the keys won't help you become the writer you want to be if you don't level up your writing and storytelling skills. This is why part 3 of this book will teach you to recognize your strengths and weaknesses in the craft and implement four techniques that can help you develop your creative abilities.

Having developed confidence, consistent practice, and the courage to seek intentional growth, part 4 of this book will at last show you how to get clear about what you really want from your writing life—what will truly bring you the creative fulfillment you crave. With that aim in mind, you'll then create a road map to guide you in the difficult journey toward personal writing success.

Each of the principles contained in this book are the result of lessons and experiences that have revolutionized my writing life since the day I chose the path of hope. They are the same truths, tools, and techniques that I've shared for nearly as long through my website, Well-Storied.com. It's been a humbling experience to see that website gain a devoted readership of fellow writers over the past five years. It's been even more humbling to know those writers have followed my journey through the writing trenches and found in it hope, assurance, and strategies for success. I'm grateful for the community of writers who have shared their own journeys with me in return.

I've spoken with writers as young as eleven and as old as ninety-two. I've made friends with storytellers worldwide, held thousands of online conversations on the craft, and learned from the experiences of writers who have cracked open their creative spirits and allowed me to slip inside the beautiful messes of their minds. With every new connection, I've learned more about the craft, the creative process, and the unique strategies that have helped writers turn their dreams into writing realities. And if I've learned one essential truth in the past five years of writing and connecting with fellow writers, it's that you are capable of becoming the writer you want to be.

So let's get to work.

PART I

THE CREATIVE MINDSET

Mindset:
> *: a mental attitude or inclination*
> *: a fixed state of mind*

—Merriam-Webster

"So this, I believe, is the central question upon which all creative living hinges: Do you have the courage to bring forth the treasures that are hidden within you?"

—Elizabeth Gilbert,
Big Magic

1

THE ROOT OF CREATIVE FRUSTRATION

It's not what you don't know that holds you back; it's what you do know that isn't true.

—Jack Canfield,
The Success Principles

All writers experience creative frustration from time to time. But what if you experience creative frustration most of the time?

If you've picked up this book, you're likely dissatisfied with your writing life in some way. Maybe you've yet to finish a first draft after years of writing, always lured by the siren song of a new story idea not long after beginning the last. Maybe you've developed an idea you love, but you're afraid of failing to do the story justice. Maybe you've been struggling to find the time or motivation to sit down and write.

Sound familiar? You aren't alone, writer.

Creative frustrations come in all shapes and sizes and can

result from a lack of time, knowledge, skill, energy, and focus. This book will tackle each of these issues in turn, but the attitude you carry with you into any creative endeavor will define both the quality of your everyday writing life and your long-term writing success. To lay the foundation for the work to come, you must first hone a healthy creative mindset.

The first step in doing so lies in addressing the underlying current that makes it so difficult to find your creative footing: resistance.

What Is Resistance?

Resistance is the antimuse. It's the feeling that stops you in your tracks when you try to put pen to paper. It's a combination of doubt, dread, and, sometimes, inexplicable indifference. Such is the power of resistance that author Steven Pressfield even refers to it in *The War of Art* with a capital *R*.

Resistance. It's one hell of a writing roadblock right out of the gate, and it lives within your mind. At its core, resistance is nothing more than fear. It's what you experience when you desire something you believe will bring immense value to your life, but you're too afraid to pursue it. With resistance, the fear of risk outweighs the potential for reward.

For writers, that reward is creative fulfillment, while the potential for risk runs far and wide. Writing itself demands a great deal of time and energy, and there's no guarantee you'll translate your vision for your project onto the page. The act of sharing the work you create then invites criticism and rejection. For some writers, creative work even brings the possibility of judgment and disapproval from those they love.

It's therefore no wonder that resistance preys upon writers' creative desires, including your own. When faced with resistance, your willpower takes one look at the dangers involved in pursuing the writing life and decides that walking you straight to the couch for a Netflix binge is a much better idea. With Netflix, there's nothing to risk, nothing to fear—or so says resistance. But in truth, what greater fear is there for a writer than to leave their stories unwritten? To never pursue the creative work that brings them so much joy?

Writer, It's Time to Fight Back

When faced with resistance, it isn't your job to defeat fear. As Steven Pressfield says in *The War of Art*, "The amateur believes he must first overcome his fear; then he can do his work. The professional knows that fear can never be overcome. He knows there is no such thing as a fearless warrior or a dread-free artist."

Pressfield couldn't be any closer to the truth. To overcome resistance isn't to defeat fear. It's to *brave* your fears. To pick up the pen despite the risks involved in doing so. To put in the difficult creative work to become the writer you want to be.

Bravery isn't an easy choice. But if you're no longer willing to accept the damage that fear inflicts, it's the right choice to make. You'll recognize this when you realize you're tired of staring down your drawer full of unfinished manuscripts or debating whether every last word you've written is the right word to use in that spot or loathing yourself for doing anything but writing. More importantly, you'll know you're ready to choose bravery when you're willing to fight to find the creative fulfillment you crave. Does this sound like you? Then it's time to face the enemy within.

The surest way to gain higher ground in the battle against resistance is to cultivate a healthy creative mindset that favors bravery. That work begins with learning to defend against resistance's primary weapon of choice: doubt.

If you're anything like the writer next door, you're full of creative doubt. But contrary to common belief, doubt isn't your creative enemy. It's a neutral force that highlights potential issues in the form of questions such as the following:

- Does that line not evoke the image I want to share?
- Have I done enough to develop that character?
- What if no one likes my story?
- Is my voice too bland?
- What if I never publish my book?
- What if I publish my book and no one buys it?

Doubt highlights the presence of uncertainty, and uncertainty will forever be part of your writing life. You can't find a clear and definite scale by which you can critique your work, nor can you divine the future, so it's natural to question the quality of your work and the potential for your projects' success.

It's natural to doubt. How you respond to doubt determines the state of your creative mindset.

The healthiest response to doubt is action. When you acknowledge the uncertainty of an issue, you can determine the best way to resolve as much of that uncertainty as possible. If you're worried a particular line in your latest chapter isn't written as smoothly or precisely as you'd like, you can rearrange the structure of the sentence or run the passage by a friend for critique. If you're worried your book won't sell when it's published, you can seek out resources that teach book launch and marketing strategies.

Activity: List Your Doubts and Brainstorm Solutions

During your next writing session, use a notebook to jot down any creative doubts that crop up. Then review your list at the end of your session, and brainstorm the actions you can take to resolve them. If you're unsure, try searching your query online or asking a fellow writer how they handle the same uncertainty.

When deciding which doubt to resolve first, you have two options. You can tackle the doubt that has the most immediate impact on your writing life, or you can tackle several doubts that are quickly resolved to ease the burden on your creative mindset.

If you find several ways in which you can resolve a particular doubt, then choose the action that's most applicable to your situation. For example, if you're worried that your character isn't well developed, you can study characterization techniques or ask for feedback from a trusted source. Studying the topic can reveal many helpful insights if you know little about characterization. On the other hand, seeking feedback is often the better choice if you're unsure of whether your character translates well on the page.

Sometimes taking action is easy. Sometimes it isn't. But when you don't take action, the alternatives are fear, stagnancy, and self-loathing. And oh, how resistance knows this.

Resistance loves to deter you from acting by convincing you that doubt is the real creative enemy—and that its presence indicates a personal failing. "Can't seem to work out your plot?" it might say. "Worried that your book won't sell? Clearly, you're an awful writer. You never should have picked up the pen."

This is the voice of resistance. And when you take resistance at its word, you alter the nature of doubt. You strip the question mark of its uncertainty and twist it into the period of a limiting belief, a conviction that restrains you from living out your full potential.

Resistance loves to whisper limiting beliefs like these in your ear:

- You can't be a writer. You aren't good enough.
- Your stories aren't original. They're too weird, too silly, too grim. No one will read them.
- Don't you know that writing is selfish? You're taking time away from your kids and your loved ones.
- You're kidding yourself if you think that writing will get you anywhere in life. Who are you to be a writer?

At some point in your life, someone spoke your limiting beliefs to you as truths. Perhaps they came from a school-teacher, parent, or friend. Or maybe you heard them in a speech or as silly one-liners on a late-night sitcom. Either way, you aren't at fault for believing these lies. It's easy to internalize limiting beliefs when they're presented as truths. But you *are* responsible for what you choose to believe going forward.

To hone a creative mindset that fosters bravery instead of fear and inaction, you must unpack the limiting beliefs that threaten your resolve. Listen to your negative self-talk. The next time resistance whispers a limiting belief in your ear, recognize that belief for the lie it is and counter it with a true statement, such as one of these:

- I'm as good a writer as I work toward being.
- My stories are original because I'm the one telling them.
- I write the stories I want to read, and that's good enough.
- I will be someone's favorite writer.

- When I pursue my passion for writing, I become a better version of myself.
- When I write, I show my children that it's good to pursue what brings them joy.
- Writing is an expression of self, and I'm worthy of being heard.
- I am a writer.

Call it an affirmation, a mantra, or a personal pep talk. When you commit to responding to your limiting beliefs with words of truth, you begin the slow but steady process of revolutionizing your creative mindset.

Activity: State Your Truth with Affirmations

Recognizing your limiting beliefs can be difficult. Pay attention to how you talk to yourself. The next time you find yourself engaging in negative self-talk, write down the limiting belief you were thinking, then list a true statement that disproves it. You can now use these true statements to oppose the call of resistance.

Repeat this practice as often as necessary, speaking your affirmations aloud to reaffirm their truth. You may find it helpful to maintain a notebook (or a note-taking app) devoted to this purpose.

You can find a list of my favorite creative affirmations at the end of this book.

As you continue the practice you built in the Affirmations activity above, you'll notice an increase in your awareness of your limiting beliefs and find it easier to reject them. In time, you'll even begin to recognize when resistance tries to twist doubts into limiting beliefs. When this happens, remember that doubt isn't your creative enemy. Rather, doubt is uncertainty. Whenever you can, take action to resolve this uncertainty. When you do, and when you choose truth over limiting beliefs, you'll strengthen the foundations of your creative mindset. You'll recognize that writing brings you immense personal reward and begin cultivating the bravery you need to fight against resistance. In other words, you'll take the first step toward becoming the writer you want to be.

2

CULTIVATING CONFIDENCE IN YOUR WRITING

No one is born a writer. You must become a writer. In fact, you never cease becoming, because you never stop learning how to write.

—Joe Bunting,
author and founder of The Write Practice

If there is a gap between where you are in your writing life and where you'd like to be, resistance will work to convince you that you aren't good enough to make the leap. But the fear that you aren't good enough is just another limiting belief, one that undermines the creative confidence you need to build your best writing life.

To become the writer you long to be, you must believe in your ability to complete difficult creative work. This might sound like a tall order, but cultivating confidence in your writing doesn't have to be as challenging as it seems. In fact, you can begin today, regardless of your current writing ability.

Developing your writing and storytelling skills is always a valuable endeavor, but don't mistake skill or experience for confidence. Improving your writing can have a positive effect on your creative self-esteem, but to truly rest assured in your abilities, you must weed out the limiting belief that you aren't good enough.

The thing is, you can't be or become a "good enough" writer, because the concept of "good enough" is subjective. Is your novel good enough to land a book deal? Who knows? Lackluster books are published alongside better crafted and more engaging reads every day. Are your stories good enough to capture readers' attention? Again, who knows? Your stories won't appeal to all readers. But if you're writing a story you want to read, it's likely that others will want to read it too.

The fact that you're questioning whether your skills and stories are good enough is a clear indicator of doubt, and the healthy response to doubt is action. But taking action against a subjective concept is a challenge in and of itself.

Many writers seek assurance in external validation to help alleviate the fear that their work isn't good enough. They look forward to the day they'll land an agent or their first five-star review, thinking it will give them the permission they need to feel confident in their skills and stories. But the trouble with seeking this kind of confidence is that it, too, is based on subjectivity. An agent might sign you as a client, but what happens when you aren't offered a book deal? Or when your book launches to little fanfare? What happens when someone counters a five-star review of your book with a harsh critique? By looking outside yourself for proof that you're good enough, you strap yourself into an emotional rollercoaster with no happy ending in sight.

To cultivate confidence in your writing, you must ditch the idea that you aren't good enough and instead seek validation from within. And the first step in this endeavor requires that you root out the underlying limiting beliefs that keep you from confident creation.

Belief 1: I'm Not Talented Enough to Be a Writer

Society loves to feed us the image of the talented artist. Having earned the favor of the muse or God above, the talented artist excels in their craft as though they were made solely for that purpose. Their work is transcendent, otherworldly. The everyman marvels at its wonder. But society's image of the talented artist is only a snapshot of the truth behind that artist's experiences. It's not the whole picture.

Indeed, people in this world have been blessed with extraordinary talent—whether by fluke of nature or divine hand, I can't say. What I do know is that talent doesn't determine success. It might be a sizable bootstrap with which to pull oneself up, but talent is not passion. It is not determination. It is not damn hard work. Talent can't succeed on its own merits. Nor is it an essential ingredient for success.

At the end of the day, you're as good a writer as you work toward being. You can learn how to tell a good story, develop effective prose, and embrace creativity as an essential part of your life. With a love for stories and the determination to improve your ability to write your own, you can become the writer you want to be. No ifs, ands, or buts about it.

Affirmation
"I'm as good a writer as I work toward being."

Belief 2: I'm Not a "Real" Writer

New writers are often reluctant to call themselves writers. Maybe you have felt this same hesitation. When it comes to creativity, no gatekeeper is there to judge whose writing is good and whose isn't. If you're writing, then you're a writer. Talent, skill, experience, publication—none of it matters in defining whether you can claim the title.

The kid popping ollies in an empty parking lot is just as much a skateboarder as legend Tony Hawk. They are both on the board, day after day, doing what they love. Your being a writer is exactly the same. You become a writer the day you decide to pick up the pen (and to keep picking it up), making you just as worthy of the title as Nora Roberts, Toni Morrison, George R. R. Martin, and other writing icons. To believe anything less is evidence of a deep-seated limiting belief.

"I can't call myself a writer," you say. "I've never finished a story." But you're working on one, aren't you? Then you're a writer. "I can't call myself a writer," you say. "I've never been published." Is a painter not a painter until they sell their first piece? The only validation you need to call yourself a writer comes from within. Are you passionate about your work? Are you putting in the time and effort to bring that work to life? Then claim your pen, writer.

This early hesitation to call yourself what you are is the first sign of Imposter Syndrome, a psychological pattern in which creatives—or anyone, for that matter—downplay their accomplishments in the fear that they'll one day be exposed as a fraud. If left unchecked, Imposter Syndrome can lead you to place undue pressure on yourself to excel at an impossible level. That pressure can then manifest as writer's block, perfectionism, fear of the blank page, and other debilitating forms of resistance. The sooner you claim the title of writer, the sooner you'll confront Imposter Syndrome as a result.

If you're already well into your writing journey and find that Imposter Syndrome is holding you back, recognize that this is simply a pattern of limiting beliefs. Fight back with words of truth that are unique to your situation, take action against your doubts, and celebrate each and every one of your creative accomplishments, no matter how big or how small. You are not a fraud. You're a writer, as real as they come.

Affirmation
"I write. Therefore, I'm a writer."

Belief 3: Writing Isn't Really My Calling

I loathe the idea that we're born with an inherent calling we're meant to discover. The concept is simply too black-and-white for my tastes. Plus, assuming that a calling is equivalent to talent can prove problematic. This leads resistance to whisper in your ear: "You aren't immediately excelling in your new interest? Well, it must not be your calling." Ick! So how do you know if the writing life is for you?

Oprah Winfrey defines passion as energy,[1] and that's a concept I can stand behind. Though I always had an interest in writing and storytelling, these avenues didn't energize me until I was seventeen, when I was tormented by the countdown to high school graduation. Desperate for escape, I turned to penning stories and never looked back.

Writing continues to energize me today for many reasons. I love the creative challenge, the excitement of developing new projects, and the pursuit of a career independent of an office cubicle. I also love the incredible community I've built with fellow writers and storytellers online. How about you? Does writing energize you for these reasons too? Or for different ones? In any case, don't wait for the heavens to part and the muse to descend, robes shimmering, to declare your calling as a writer. If writing energizes you, then write.

Granted, the day-to-day act of writing can be draining. Remember that writing is hard work. It frequently demands much of your mental and emotional energy. When considering your passion, look for energy in the big picture instead. Does the challenge of writing a book excite you? Then go write one! Do you have a story idea you're eager to share with the rest of the world? Then it's time to get to work!

Affirmation
"Writing energizes and excites me. Therefore, I will write."

Cultivate True Creative Confidence

Confidence can't be found in external validation or in developing your skills and stories until you're "good enough." You must look inward to cultivate confidence in your writing, but confronting your limiting beliefs is only half the battle. Replacing limiting beliefs with words of truth can only help you if you recognize that confidence is not a state of being you can attain. It's faith—faith in your ability to complete difficult creative work and bring your stories to life.

Remember that nothing is certain in the writing life. Doubt is inevitable, and fear will be your daily foe. One day, you might realize you've developed the confidence you need in your skills and stories. However, many well-established writers confess to making a conscious effort to place faith in their abilities every day. "The problem is that bad writers tend to have the self-confidence," said Charles Bukowski in *Sunlight Here I Am: Interviews and Encounters, 1963–1993*, "while the good ones tend to have self-doubt." The reason for this lies in the nature of doubt, which highlights areas of uncertainty.

Bad writers rarely feel uncertain. They believe their work is beyond reproach and therefore entitled to praise from readers, critics, and industry professionals. But no writer should aspire to confidence born out of arrogance. Good writers are good writers *because* they heed their doubts. Uncertainty breeds humility, and with a healthy creative mindset, humility allows good writers to view their doubts as opportunities for growth.

In striving to resolve their doubts, good writers become better writers over time. This is how you can find confidence in your creativity: by placing faith in your ability to become the writer you want to be.

The work ahead will be difficult. At times, you might even believe it's impossible to bridge the gap between where you are in your writing life and where you want to be. But confident writers know they can make the leap despite this limiting belief. That if they never stop studying the craft and developing their skills, they will never cease becoming better writers.

Good writers excel because they write from a place of humility. They recognize that growth is uncomfortable work, and they settle into that discomfort, empowered by the knowledge that they are forever capable of improving in their craft.

Are you willing to put in that same work? Are you ready to never cease *becoming*?

∽

Activity: Cultivate Confidence with a Daily Affirmation

If you struggle to believe you're a capable writer, open a notebook and write the following sentence: "I am becoming the writer I want to be." Make a habit of writing (or verbalizing) this affirmation every day, especially before and during your writing sessions. Let it empower you to choose confidence in the face of fear. Any time you doubt your ability, go back to the List Your Doubts and Brainstorm Solutions activity in chapter 1.

∽

3

OWNING YOUR ORIGINALITY

In life, finding a voice is speaking and living the truth. Each of you is an original. Each of you has a distinctive voice. When you find it, your story will be told. You will be heard.

—John Grisham,
best-selling author of more than
thirty-five legal thrillers

Originality is an essential ingredient in storytelling. Without it, you cannot create. You can only duplicate. But when you own your originality, you allow your vibrant creative spirit to thrive. You distinguish yourself from fellow writers and craft memorable stories that resonate with readers —readers who return to your books time and time again because they love your work.

Recognizing the power of originality, resistance will discourage you from embracing it. It may insist that your work is too derivative, or that your unconventional stories could never appeal to readers. It may even insist that you sanitize your writing to avoid disappointing or offending others. The thing is, you can't own your originality without writing the stories you want to share.

Each of these creative worries indicates the presence of much deeper fears: the fears of criticism, rejection, and judgment. Resistance knows it can use these fears to suppress what makes your work unique until your doubts turn into limiting beliefs that leave you too terrified to write. If this sounds familiar, then know that you aren't alone. Fear might be your constant creative companion, but remember that it isn't your job to defeat fear. It's your job to be brave despite the fear that resistance throws your way.

To make space for your creative spirit to thrive, let's first dig into what lies at the root of these common creative fears.

Fear of Criticism: "My Stories Aren't Original Enough"

One of the quickest ways that resistance can use originality as a weapon against creative progress is by skewing what *originality* really means. If resistance can convince you that your work must be wholly new and previously unimagined to be original, then it's sure to stop you in your tracks, because nothing in this world is new. No story on this earth hasn't been explored, flipped, reimagined, retold, mashed up, or broken down.

In truth, your work is original regardless of what you write because *you* are the one writing it. No one has your mind or imagination. No one shares your exact upbringing, experiences, interests, world view, personality, or beliefs—and each of these factors plays a role in forming your unique writing voice.

This blend of your identity, opinions, and background is what makes your work original. If you take what you love from the stories you consume, mix them with additional sources of inspiration, and write all of it down in the voice that only you possess, you *will* craft original stories. Even if you're creating work that builds heavily on what's come before, such as fan fiction or genre fiction, your stories are original because *you* are the one writing them.

If you're worried that your work is derivative, I'd wager that what you truly fear is criticism. Will someone read your work, find the faint trail of inspiration, and call you out for stealing someone else's idea? So long as you aren't plagiarizing or putting just a slight spin on another author's work, let this criticism roll right off. You can't please everyone.

Besides, all work is derivative, including the classics. J. R. R. Tolkien didn't invent elves, dwarves, and goblins. He borrowed them from mythology, just as Stephen King found inspiration for *It* in folktales and children's fairy stories. Jane Austen made use of themes and character archetypes that were typical in other novels of her time. Suzanne Collins hearkened back to Roman gladiatorial games in her novel *The Hunger Games*, and Disney's *The Lion King* borrowed its core narrative from Shakespeare's *Hamlet*. Yet each of these stories stands apart from others because of the unique voices of their authors.

In the end, if you know you've written the story you want to tell in the way that only you can tell it, then keep writing. Criticism that comments on a lack of originality says far more about the critic than it does about you.

Affirmation
"My work is original because I am the one writing it."

Fear of Rejection: "My Stories Are Too Unconventional to Attract Readers"

Most writers write commercial fiction, stories that fall within clear-cut genres and stick to conventions that sell. Why do those conventions sell? Because readers enjoy them. For some writers, knowing this can lead to the fear that their work might be too original, too "out there," to interest potential readers—another fear that resistance loves to seize upon. But even if you think your creative interests are uncommon, know that you aren't the only one who finds them fascinating. If you're writing the book you want to read, others will want to read it too.

Will more readers pick up a murder mystery than a romance set on Mars or a fantasy novel written from a dragon's perspective? Probably. But you aren't looking to please all readers, or even a large number of them. You're looking for readers who share your interests so you can get your books into their hands. This search might sound difficult, but finding your readership may be easier than you'd expect. Just think of how many odd ideas have inspired cult-classic books, films, television shows, comics, and even mainstream best-sellers.

Consider the Outlander series by Diana Gabaldon, in which a World War II combat nurse travels back in time to the eighteenth century, falls in love with a Scottish outlaw, and attempts to stop the third Jacobite Rebellion. Or Neil Gaiman's *American Gods*, in which a newly released prisoner finds himself mixed up in a battle between the old gods of mythology and the new gods of technology, media, and globalization. Or Jasper Fforde's *The Eyre Affair*, in which a literary detective named Thursday Next follows a terrorist into the pages of Charlotte Brontë's *Jane Eyre* to stop him from using the threat of literary destruction to blackmail important public figures.

Yes, "weird" can be a great selling point. So write what you love, then find the readers who will love what you've written. No story is too unconventional to make its mark.

Affirmation
"Every story, including my own, has an audience."

Fear of Judgment: "I Can't Write What I Want to Write"

You can't own your originality if you aren't writing what you want to write. Yet doing so can be challenging when faced with judgment from family members, friends, or acquaintances—or even your own judgments about yourself.

The latter is the easier judgment to conquer. If you aren't telling the stories you want to tell because you believe they're in some way not good enough, recognize this for the limiting belief that it is. Literary fiction isn't inherently better than commercial fiction because it holds literary merit. Nor is commercial fiction the better choice to write because it's more conventionally marketable and entertaining. Every genre and subgenre have readers. So do quirky and introspective literary tales and upmarket stories that fall somewhere between the two extremes.

If you want to write it, then write it. Your story matters.

When it comes to judgment from the people in your life, you'll need to accept a hard truth: your worst fears might be reality. The types of stories you write might disappoint or offend those around you, even those you love. My stories often explore themes such as sex and sexuality, violence, mental illness, and abuse—themes that would appall some of my family members. I'd be lying if I said I didn't fear the day when one of them reads my work. But I can't change the opinions of others, and I won't cheapen my creative fulfillment to tailor my writing to someone else's ideal.

Whenever fear weighs heavy on me, I return to this passage from Austin Kleon's *Steal Like an Artist*: "Not everybody will get it. People will misinterpret you and what you do. They might even call you names. So get comfortable with being misunderstood, disparaged, or ignored—the trick is to be too busy doing your work to care."

Remember that you can't control what others think of you

or your work. Some of them might even judge you for your decision to write in the first place. But to build a writing life you love, you'll need to prioritize your creative interests and pursuits over others' opinions. Create the work you want to create, and you'll love the writing life you lead.

Affirmation
"I deserve to write what I love regardless of what others think."

Without owning your originality, it's impossible to thrive in the writing life you're building. Your fears of criticism, rejection, and judgment will hinder you time and time again until you have little desire to pick up the pen. But you know how to fight these fears. You know how to look your limiting beliefs in the face and recognize them for what they are, using words of truth to transform your mindset into a powerhouse for creative pursuits. Seize this knowledge, and take action. Ignore anyone who judges your interests, and celebrate what makes your work unique.

When you write the stories you want to write in the way that only you can write them, you empower yourself to build a writing life you love.

～

Activity: Identify What Makes Your Work Unique

To uncover your writing voice, open a notebook and create a list for each of the following:

- Your interests
- Your most memorable and defining experiences
- Your values and beliefs
- Your attitude and personality traits

- Story elements you love

Here are a few examples that represent my own writing voice. Each of these elements plays a role in the stories I develop:

- **Interests:** astronomy, medieval history, mythology
- **Experiences:** situational depression, emotional abuse, rebelling against family expectations
- **Values and Beliefs:** social equality and inclusion, radical kindness, generosity
- **Attitude and Personality:** introverted, ambitious, highly curious
- **Story Elements:** romance, sword fights, bittersweet endings

After creating your lists, consider how you can include these elements in your work to craft truly original stories.

4

THE ONLY WAY TO DO THE DAMN
HARD WORK

Don't change your self-criticism habit. Change your habitual reactions to self-criticism.

—Yong Kang Chan, *The Disbelief Habit*

Resistance has a nasty habit of taking opportunities and convincing you that they are roadblocks. It does this by turning doubts into limiting beliefs and persuading you that your inner critic is the enemy. But self-criticism isn't the bane of creativity that resistance would have you believe it is. In fact, your inner critic is key to your development as a writer.

If you had no inner critic, you would write without doubt. This reality might sound appealing at first, but remember that doubts are essential to growth. Without them, you wouldn't question the quality of your work or seek to improve your writing and storytelling skills. You'd write from a place of arrogance, believing your work to be beyond reproach. As first discussed in chapter 2, writers who work in this attitude of entitlement and conceit rarely achieve any measure of success in their writing lives. Something tells me that isn't what you want for your creative work.

Building a positive relationship with your inner critic is the final foundational key to honing a healthy creative mindset, but navigating self-criticism can be difficult because it introduces doubt. Without knowing how to resolve doubt with action, writers often fear and repress their inner critics—or, worse, allow resistance to kick that inner critic into overdrive. Both of these reactions result from fear. Fear of judgment, fear of criticism, fear of rejection, or even the fear of failure: the belief that you aren't good enough to become the writer you want to be.

We've discussed each of these fears in the first three chapters of this book. But when dealing with the inner critic, resistance loves to use these fears to warp healthy self-criticism into two common creative roadblocks: perfectionism and the comparison trap.

How Perfectionism Can Harm Your Writing Life

As a writer, one of the hardest truths to accept is that the story you wrestle onto the page will never fully reflect the story in your head and your heart. It will fall short, at least in some way. You might even look back on your work several years later and find yourself humbled—and perhaps embarrassed—by your early creative efforts. Such shortcomings are inevitable, but I don't say this to be demoralizing. It's simply a reality you must accept if you're to find fulfillment in your writing life.

When you chase perfection, you chase an impossible ideal. Great writers are still human and fallible, and they recognize there's always room for improvement in their skills and stories. More importantly, they don't let that reality stop them from finishing and sharing their work.

Resistance would have you believe that the pursuit of

perfection results from chasing self-improvement, but that's not the case. As Brené Brown writes in *The Gifts of Imperfection*, a healthy inner critic is self-interested—in other words, it strives for self-improvement because it knows that growth is fulfilling work—whereas the inner perfectionist is others-centered. It seeks approval, constantly fearing what others will think.

Perfectionism insists that what you do and how well you do it determines your self-worth. This, however, is one of the most damaging limiting beliefs. No amount of success or external praise can give you self-esteem. That assurance must always come from within, from the full belief that you're worthy simply because you exist.

Affirmation

"I acknowledge my intrinsic self-worth.
I am more than the work I create."

When it comes to creative pursuits, perfectionism will insist that if you strive hard enough, you can create work that is beyond reproach. But this is just another limiting belief. No matter how hard you strive, you can't avoid criticism, because the quality of creative work is subjective. One reader will love a story that another reader won't bother to finish and a third reader will rip to shreds in a scathing review. If you allow your fear of this reality to outweigh your love for your work, you'll never finish a single story. You will kill your writing dreams before you take the first step toward achieving them.

Instead, commit to creating imperfect work. Get the first draft down, regardless of how it reads. Then revise your story to the best of your ability, and send it out for critical feedback. Work on polishing your prose without interrogating every last comma and word choice. An imperfect story is always more enjoyable than one that is never finished.

Affirmation

"I will write happily and freely because done is better than perfect."

Many writers who struggle with perfectionism use timed writing sessions and draft deadlines to push past their nit-picking as they work on uprooting their limiting beliefs. Others find it helpful to work with a book coach or critique partner who can hold them accountable for finishing their work. The fear of disappointing an ally cheering for your success can help you overcome the fear of facing criticism over your work.

Activity: Set a Session Goal

The next time you sit down for a writing session, set a deadline-oriented goal like one of these to encourage progress over perfectionism:

- Draft five hundred words in thirty minutes
- Revise five pages in one hour

Time-sensitive goals based around output won't work for every writer, but they can provide the healthy pressure you need to curb your overactive inner critic and get words on the page.

Are You Caught in the Comparison Trap?

Call it comparisonitis, the comparison game, or plain old envy. When you haven't cultivated confidence in your creative abilities, resistance will urge your inner critic to take one look at other writers' work and find your own lacking. This often leads to a deluge of doubt that can overwhelm you with fear and indecision and keep you from writing.

The comparison trap is a deadly creative roadblock because it's built on the belief that there is a "right" way to be a writer. This couldn't be further from the truth. Creativity is creativity precisely because it results from originality and innovation. There is no best story, writing style, publishing path, or creative process. There is only the best work you can create and the practices that best enable you to write and share your stories with the world.

It's okay to study other writers' careers or creative habits and consider whether their choices will help you succeed in your own. But the second you allow your inner critic to believe that another writer's choices are inherently better than yours, you usher resistance into the heart of your writing life. To sidestep the comparison trap, practice an affirmation that cuts straight to the heart of this limiting belief.

Affirmation

"I am my own writer, and I trust in my ability to make the best decisions for my skills, stories, and long-term writing success."

Like with perfectionism, you can use a few external strategies to reinforce the inner work of avoiding the comparison trap. First, let's contend with the triggers that launch you headfirst into unhealthy comparison.

Activity: Set Boundaries Around Your Comparison Triggers

The next time resistance tempts you into unhealthy comparison, acknowledge this reality and the emotions it presents. Take note of what triggered you to compare yourself to other writers, then set boundaries around how you engage with that trigger in the future. Here are three examples:

"That author's social media feed preys upon my insecurities. I'll unfollow them."

"As I write my first draft, I'll avoid reading books that are too similar to my own."

"I'll refrain from visiting websites that promote paid resources that claim to teach the only way to writing success."

Second, as both a writer and a reader, you can't avoid other authors' work. Instead, try to view their work with objectivity. If you envy an author's writing style, step back and consider whether adopting their style is truly best for your story. If an author is experiencing incredible success, explore the choices they made in their journey and see what you can glean that might apply to your own.

Finally, don't mistake action in the face of comparison as a good way to avoid the comparison trap. Resistance knows that rational choices aren't made overnight. If it can't use comparison to make you quit, it will encourage you to take immediate action that isn't right for you or your stories. If a writer's work prompts you to make a change in your own, sit with that idea for at least a week. Look at the action you're considering with objectivity, and research or reflect on whatever you need to determine your best route forward.

Embrace Your True Inner Critic

Once you've empowered yourself by establishing a healthy creative mindset, your inner critic will present you with opportunities for growth in your writing life. It will seek self-improvement, not destruction, and be empowered by the confidence you've cultivated in your ability to become the writer you want to be. And as you take the next steps in your writing journey, you're going to need both your inner critic and your confidence.

Building your best writing life is a long, hard slog. Throughout these first four chapters, you've completed difficult *internal* work that has established a strong foundation for the difficult *external* work to come. And make no mistake—there's a lot of damn hard work in your future. But that work will be worth the effort when you actively progress toward becoming the writer you long to be.

The remainder of this book will help you form a personalized writing practice that works with your schedule and creative process, harness tools for the intentional development of your writing and storytelling skills, and plan your road map to personal writing success. All of this requires a healthy relationship with your inner critic and confidence in your ability to fulfill the opportunities for self-improvement that your inner critic presents.

This isn't easy work, especially with the host of obstacles and uncertainties that will crop up on your path to writing success. Never mind the fact that resistance will always be close behind. It's no wonder that Steven Pressfield writes in *The War of Art* that "the artist committing himself to his calling has volunteered for hell, whether he knows it or not. He will be dining for the duration on a diet of isolation, rejection, self-doubt, despair, ridicule, contempt, and humiliation."

Your writing life is meant to be full of immense joy and incredible creative fulfillment, but the process of building your best writing life will be a challenge, and certain trials will remain a fixture in that writing life. Are you willing to push through the pain in pursuit of your passion? Then rest assured that the healthy creative mindset you've honed will carry you through each step in your writing journey.

PART II

THE WRITING PRACTICE

Practice:

: a repeated or customary action

: the condition of being proficient through systematic exercise

—Merriam-Webster

We first make our habits, and then our habits make us.

—John Dryden

5

INSPIRATION, MOTIVATION, AND THE POWER OF CREATIVE HABIT

Habit will sustain you whether you're inspired or not. Habit will help you finish and polish your stories. Inspiration won't. Habit is persistence in practice.

—Octavia Butler,
Hugo and Nebula Award-winning
science fiction author

There's nothing like the writing flow, when inspiration strikes and words seem to spring from your fingertips onto the page. These are the moments in which you lose yourself to the glory of creation, in which writing makes you feel even more alive.

After tasting this vibrant creative energy, you might find yourself hooked on inspiration, chasing it day after day as you begin your writing journey. But what happens when the muse suddenly vanishes? If you're motivated by inspiration alone, then you'll struggle to put words on the page, and that struggle will result in increasing frustration that opens the door to the pull of resistance. It's no wonder that writers who rely upon the muse to inspire their work often fail to finish their stories.

If you want to build a writing life you love, then you cannot treat inspiration as an unreliable mystical power that exists separate from yourself. In truth, inspiration is a biological phenomenon—a powerful source of creativity that lives within your mind. Why, then, is inspiration often fleeting?

The Truth About Inspiration

The subconscious part of your mind is constantly at work, mulling over the vast amount of information you feed it every day. When your subconscious conjures an idea or solution it deems worthy of your attention, it shoves this information to the forefront of your mind, and *boom!* You're inspired. (We'll talk more about how this process works in chapter 18.)

This revelation—a mash-up of information your subconscious has held captive—results in a flurry of motivation. Suddenly, you have a new set of characters to explore, a new scene to write, or a solution to that plot hole that's been driving you batty. With new ideas at hand, you throw yourself into your work, writing, revising, or otherwise producing work in a mad flurry of creative stimulation.

This kind of creative work is a brilliant, breathtaking experience. Yet a lack of inspiration shouldn't be lamented. If you were inspired all of the time, you'd be too busy fighting for air under the crush of new ideas to ever write a single word. This is actually a common occurrence among writers. Often called Shiny New Idea Syndrome, this overwhelm of creative stimulation can lead to a harrowing battle against distraction. If you've struggled to finish a manuscript as new story ideas fought for your attention, you know exactly what I mean.

Fortunately, inspiration can be fleeting, and this can free up energy for you to focus on finishing one project at a time. But where can you source creative energy if it doesn't stem from inspiration?

The Two Main Types of Creative Energy

The trouble with inspiration is that it's the sugar high of creative energy. Tasting the power that comes from crafting something out of nothing can be an addictive experience, but inspiration strikes hard and then retreats, leading to a crash in creative energy.

Hooked on the high that inspiration provides, many writers make the mistake of waiting for the muse to arrive before writing, a practice that often has the opposite of its intended effect. The less frequently you write, the more you'll teach your subconscious to devalue your creative work and encourage it to spend less time brewing new ideas. As a result, you'll struggle to make progress because you haven't trained your brain to write on a consistent basis.

This stagnancy often becomes a playground for resistance. "What's wrong with me?" you might ask. "Why do I feel so inspired one day and so depleted the next? How do so many writers maintain their routines? Where do they find the energy to keep on writing?" The answers to these questions are rooted in self-discipline—which, for writers, manifests as a consistent creative habit. A writing practice, if you will.

Think of your writing life as a marathon of the mind. Inspiration provides enough energy for a sprint, but self-discipline will drive you to the page day after day, mile after mile.

A writing practice might not sound as exciting as the wonders of the muse. If anything, the topic of self-discipline calls to mind abandoned exercise routines and fad diets gone wrong. But here's the good news: a creative habit can prove just as addictive as inspiration, if not more so. While discipline can be difficult to build, it leads to steady progress, lending a personal sense of pride and fulfillment that can only strengthen your motivation to sit down and write.

Why Is Habit a Better Source of Creative Energy?

Here's the thing about habit: when it's well established, it's self-sustaining. It doesn't rely on external sources or coincidence to exist. It becomes a fully integrated part of your everyday life, the same as going to work or brushing your teeth. Better yet, habit rarely bends to the will of resistance.

Mind you, resistance never goes away. You're in this fight for the long haul. But with a well-established writing practice, the act of writing will become second nature. You won't question whether you should sit down to write. You'll put your butt in the chair and your fingers on the keys and run another mile in your marathon of the mind.

On days when inspiration strikes, harness it and write like the wind. It might not be a sustainable source of creative energy, but it's a powerful source nonetheless. Use inspiration when it comes to call, and whenever you wake up to find that the flow of your subconscious has become stagnant, fall back on the writing practice you'll establish in the next chapter. That means sitting down and doing the work. Finishing another chapter. Writing another page. Becoming the writer you want to be.

~

Activity: Dig to the Root of Demotivation

Do you struggle to find the motivation to write? If so, open a notebook and spend a few minutes exploring the *why* behind your struggle. Be honest with yourself here. Do you believe that inspiration is essential for writing? Do you hold any limiting beliefs that have you convinced you're incapable of doing the damn hard work? Are you unsure of what to write next? Or have you written so much that you've burned through all of your creative energy?

Don't worry if you uncover an issue you don't know how to resolve. I tackle each of these motivation issues—and more —throughout the following section of the book.

6

BUILDING A SUSTAINABLE WRITING PRACTICE

In the chaos of everyday life, it's easy to lose sight of what really matters, and I can use my habits to make sure that my life reflects my values.

—Gretchen Rubin,
Better Than Before

I f you want to be a writer, you have to write. No shortcut circumvents that reality. But in the busyness of modern life, it can be difficult to focus on what you find most important. In the midst of this chaos, forging habits that enable the activities you value most can help you lead the life you desire.

If you place a high value on writing as a form of creativity and self-expression, then you'll want to build a habit that empowers you to become the writer you want to be. But writing is easier said than done, isn't it?

If you're reading this book, you know that writing is difficult. It's the reason you're looking to become a better writer.

You're frustrated by your seeming inability to sit down and write, or you're actively writing but find yourself unhappy with the progress you're making. Maybe you experience a day of exuberant creation now and then, but more often than not, you feel stuck. You've been working on your book forever or flip-flopping between a dozen story ideas, and you're tired. You just want to find a little joy in your writing life. You want to tell your stories. Why can't you do the work?

Let me reassure you, friend: you aren't a failure. You're battling resistance—and the beautiful thing about habit is that it's one of your greatest weapons against resistance.

Winning your inner creative battles requires an immense amount of willpower, but maintaining a well-established habit doesn't. By making writing a part of your weekly routine, you sidestep the brunt of resistance and free up willpower to devote to your projects. But make no mistake: some aspects of writing will continue to be difficult once you've built your practice. You'll still have to work out those plot holes and find the right words to express yourself. But how many books have never been written simply because their authors struggled to get started?

Resistance debilitates. Habit, on the other hand, empowers. Let's empower your craft by building a consistent writing practice.

How to Build a Sustainable Writing Practice

The power of daily writing has been professed from what seems like every hilltop. Even Stephen King, one of the world's most successful and prolific authors, touts the practice in his memoir of the craft, *On Writing*: "I like to get ten pages a day, which amounts to 2,000 words. That's 180,000 words over a three-month span, a goodish length for a book." But the writing habit that enables King's success—or any other writer's—may not be the best practice for you.

For some writers, the advice to write daily is dangerous and problematic. It fails to take into account the differences in writers' daily lives and the many ways in which they're wired.

In *Better Than Before*, Gretchen Rubin divides those who work toward breaking bad habits into two categories: moderators and abstainers. Moderators find it easier to build better or healthier habits when they allow themselves to "cheat" from time to time. Abstainers, on the other hand, find it less stressful to fulfill the mission of a new habit when they never again engage in the old.

In my experience, this same principle applies to writers and their routines. If not writing is your old habit and consistent writing is your new, you need to know yourself well enough to determine (or take the time to discover) whether daily writing is a help or a hindrance to the sustainability of your writing practice.

Some wiggle room exists between these two extremes. Personally, I'm an abstainer. I find it easier to write every day. However, I'm not so strict that I don't allow myself a day off when I'm ill or stressed. But I always make a point of returning to my writing the next day.

What works for me might not work for you, and that's okay. You might find it best to write on weekdays, on specific days of the week, or whenever the opportunity arises. Remember that you're aiming to build a *sustainable* writing practice, not one designed for bragging rights. Daily writing might seem ideal, but not if it sets an unattainable personal standard or frequently leads to burnout.

Still, the more consistency you can build into your writing life, the stronger your practice will be. Consistency builds habit, and habit is the source of creative energy you're looking to employ. But you don't need to execute your writing practice perfectly to reap the benefits of consistency. A good habit never leads to unhealthy pressure and stress.

So don't worry if you miss a few days of writing due to your travel schedule for work, or if you need time off from writing because of your chronic illness. If you're trying to write consistently but your kids sometimes interrupt, give yourself a little grace. Life isn't always conducive to consistency, so you have to make your writing practice work for you. It's good to establish boundaries, but it's equally important to remain flexible. If you can't bend in your creative practice when you need to, you'll break—and there's nothing sustainable about a broken writing habit.

The Truth About First Writing Efforts

Here's another hard truth about writing—and life—that you must accept in order to become the writer you want to be: the first time you do anything, the result of your effort won't be great.

It's true that you're as good a writer as you work toward being, but the blank page can be intimidating. It demands you fill it with the best you have to offer, but what the blank page doesn't share is that your best efforts are given over time.

Before you can present your best book to the world, you must polish the rough edges of your best revision. And before that, you must rewrite and reassemble your best story. And even before that, you must write the best first draft that you're able to write.

But first drafts don't need to be pretty to represent your best work. They simply need to exist. This is what you must remember when, despite resistance, you open a notebook or new document with the intention to build your writing practice. Resistance will insist that you fill the blank page with nothing but the best words you've ever written. It knows which limiting beliefs have hampered your creative endeavors in the past, and it will bring back those lies to haunt you until you question your ability to become the writer you want to be. Resistance is here to win, and it's taking no prisoners.

To claim the battle, you must fling yourself into the trenches of writing, again and again, day after day, until you're covered from head to toe in the rich clay of creativity and discover it to be a camouflage. Resistance will forever remain, lurking in the shadows, waiting for a moment to strike. But by working consistently on your practice, you'll take the upper hand.

～

Activity: Determine Your Writing Schedule

To begin building your writing practice, decide when you will write. Every day? On certain days of the week? Whenever you drop the kids off at their grandparents'? You can also establish any further boundaries, such as where you'll write and during what time of day. (We'll discuss these and similar boundaries in depth in chapter 8.)

The process of building your writing practice should be just as sustainable as the practice itself. If your routine wasn't consistent before, then don't expect to complete hour-long writing sessions right away. Instead, choose a goal you can easily attain, such as five minutes of free-writing or 100 written words. Then get to work, completing this goal for several sessions in a row. When you find yourself itching for more, increase your goal in small increments (e.g., ten minutes or 250 words). Repeat this process until you've built an ideal writing practice you can sustain.

～

7

THE KEY TO MAKING TIME TO WRITE

How many pages have I produced? I don't care. Are they any good?
I don't even think about it. All that matters is I've put in my time
and hit it with all I've got.

—Steven Pressfield,
The War of Art

Time. In this busy modern age, it feels like you're always fighting the clock. You know it's essential to make time to write. You can't maintain a consistent writing practice without carving out time in your schedule for creative work. But how are you supposed to make that time when you have a career, a family, a home, and other responsibilities to address?

Stop Looking for Time to Write

I dislike the concept of free time. If such a thing exists, it would imply that "captive time" exists as well. But who exactly is holding your time captive? You have responsibilities in life, but are your responsibilities truly dictating your time? Not at all. You might not like your day job, but you choose to go to work because you want to pay the bills, just as you choose to write that essay or change another dirty diaper. You risk something very important if you don't do it.

This is all that defines a priority: a task deemed more important than another because of the potential consequences of leaving it unfulfilled. What leaves you feeling stuck isn't a lack of choice in your priorities. Rather, it's the choice to fulfill priorities based on need before those based on desire. You do this because it's in your best interest or in the interests of those you love, even if the resulting circumstances aren't ideal.

I won't tell you that making time to write is simply a matter of wanting it enough. Common advice on this topic states that if writing is truly a priority for you, you'll make the time, and that statement can be true if taken at face value. But unless you make your living as a writer, writing likely isn't your top priority. It might be a passion, but whether it's a priority will depend on a variety of factors, including financial stability, degree of independence, physical and emotional well-being, and where writing falls in your hierarchy of desires.

I can't decide for you whether writing can or should be a priority in your life. What I can tell you, though, is that making time to write isn't a matter of carving out more free time. Your time isn't captive. You are its master—and only you get to decide how to spend it.

If your need-based priorities outweigh your desire to write, go ahead and take care of them. Then seek what solutions you can to make space for your creativity later on. If you have other desires that you want to fulfill besides writing, then don't hesitate to pursue those interests. You only have one life to live. Spend it doing what you love.

However, if you have time to read this book, then you likely have the time and desire to write, so here are five principles to help you make a more conscious effort to prioritize your writing.

Principle 1: Know Your Time

Prioritizing writing often means making at least one other activity in your life less of a priority. This is something you can't achieve unless you're aware of how you're spending your time. Take some time now to evaluate your daily and weekly activities.

Ask Yourself
"Which need-based priorities serve as the foundation of my schedule? Which desire-based priorities fill in the gaps?"

Remember that a priority is a task you deem more important than another. You might not like spending so much time on social media, but if it's filling the gaps in your schedule, it's a priority because you made it so.

To better understand how you spend your time, create a list of the top five to ten activities that fill your schedule. If you're unsure, you might benefit from tracking your activity for a few days or weeks. Laura Vanderkam, an author who explores time management, offers a great downloadable time tracker at her website LauraVanderkam.com.

Principle 2: Be Ruthless

You likely can't ignore your need-based priorities without negative consequences. But if you haven't put good habits into practice, you might be filling the remaining time in your schedule with activities that don't truly align with your values.

Ask Yourself

"Is writing a desire I truly wish to prioritize? If so, what other desires am I willing to limit or sacrifice to make more time to write?"

If you're happy with the desire-based priorities that currently fill your time, you don't need to cull them from your schedule. It's true that social media, television, video games, and similar activities receive a bad rap where time management is concerned. But social media can be a great tool for connecting with loved ones or like-minded people (hello, writing community!), and television and video games are often fantastic storytelling mediums to study. Never mind the fact that making time to relax with entertaining activities is an important part of self-care.

That being said, you only have so much time in your schedule and so much energy to give on any particular day. You might need to cull activities from your schedule that you genuinely enjoy to make time for the activity you like best: writing.

Principle 3: Set Boundaries

It's normal to be busy. But be aware that busyness can cause the lines between priorities to blur. A quick moment spent browsing social media after dinner can easily turn into the hour you meant to spend writing. To stay true to your priorities, set boundaries that protect your writing practice.

Ask Yourself

"Which activities distract me from priorities such as writing? What boundaries can I set around these activities to limit their potential for distraction?"

Personally, I'm easily tempted by online distractions like

YouTube and Netflix. While some writers find it easier to cut these distractions altogether, I allow myself to indulge in these activities only after I complete my daily to-do list.

In some cases, other *people* might distract you from writing. When this happens, politely request that they honor your writing time, but bear in mind that you can't control others' actions. Focus instead on cultivating time in ways that are firmly within your control.

Principle 4: Play to Your Process

Every writer's process is unique. Therefore, the only right way to structure your writing time is the way that works best for you. The common advice to write every day, which was introduced in chapter 6, might work for you—but it also might not. The same goes for other popular suggestions, such as writing whenever you have ten minutes to spare (it all adds up!) or only when you have a large block of time to dedicate to your work.

Each of these approaches will work well for different writers. To utilize your schedule wisely, first discover the approach that works best for you—a topic we'll discuss in chapter 9— then structure your writing time in a way that honors your unique process.

Ask Yourself

"Do I work best in small or large blocks of time? Based on this knowledge, how can I best schedule writing time into my week? How can I make it easier to write when I have the time to work according to my process?"

Principle 5: Find Balance

Writing can be demanding. It requires mental and emotional effort that isn't always easy to muster, especially if you aren't taking care of yourself. To maintain a consistent writing practice, try to find balance between your creative work and other important aspects of your life. Spend time with your kids. Get some fresh air, read a book, or call a friend. Reduce unnecessary stress by prioritizing needs over desires. When you nourish yourself and your relationships, you can put your best effort into your creative work.

Ask Yourself

"What aspects of my life matter most to me? What activities do I find nourishing when I'm feeling physically, mentally, or emotionally drained? Based on what I know about myself, how can I reorder my schedule to find more balance in my life?"

Making time to write is key to developing a sustainable writing habit, but it's okay to practice flexibility when necessary. If you need an extended break to care for yourself or fulfill other priorities, then go ahead and give yourself that break. Your stories will be right there waiting for you when you're ready to return to them.

Finally, remember that good time management is a muscle that must be strengthened and maintained. It's unrealistic to expect to overhaul your habits overnight. Instead, focus on slow and steady improvement. Can you carve out five minutes each day to write? How about one hour a week? Fantastic! Work toward that goal until you can do so with little resistance. Then, when you feel comfortable, increase your goal to ten minutes, two hours, or whatever time interval works best for you.

All progress is good progress. Big writing gains might seem more productive in the short term, but patience and persistence are the true keys to long-term creative success. Are you willing to put in the time to build a writing practice you can sustain?

8

CLAIMING YOUR CREATIVE WORKSPACE

To get the creative habit, you need a working environment that's habit-forming.

—Twyla Tharp,
The Creative Habit

Consistency is critical for building a writing practice that circumvents resistance and promotes measurable progress. But consistency isn't limited to how frequently you write. The better you come to know yourself as a creator, the more consistency you can build into all aspects of your writing life, including the "where" and "how."

In the next chapter, I'll show you how to rock your personal writing process by uncovering techniques that will help you consistently produce your best work. But first, it's time to claim your creative space, the atmosphere in which you do your best work. This consists of more than just the physical conditions that define your personal writing workspace. It's also the mental space that fosters clarity and focus and the habit triggers that make it easier than ever to maintain a consistent writing practice. Let's dig into how you can define these three facets of your ideal creative space.

Define Your Personal Writing Workspace

It's not where or how you create that's most important, but rather what you create with the time, circumstances, and energy available to you. That said, don't undervalue the power of making a distinct creative workspace (or at least a set of physical conditions) in which you can create your best work.

∼

Activity: Create Your Personal Writing Workspace

Use the prompts on the following pages to define the physical conditions that are most conducive to your writing practice.

∼

Location: Is there a specific place where you do your best creative work? I prefer solitude so I can read my work aloud, so you'll usually find me sitting at my writing desk at home. Other writers prefer working in other spots at home (the kitchen table, a comfy sofa) or away from home altogether (a coffee shop, the library, outdoors).

Time: At what time of day do you feel most creative? At what time are there fewer distractions in your schedule? Do these times intersect, thus creating the ideal opportunity to write? I feel most creative at night, after the rush of the day has ended. Evenings are also the perfect time in my schedule for my fiction projects, since I spend all day creating books and resources for writers.

Sound: Do you need complete silence to produce your best work? (I do!) Do you love listening to music playlists you create that remind you of your characters or stories? Or do you enjoy working to the hum of the television on low volume, the chatter of customers at a café, or the sounds produced by a white noise app or machine?

Comfort: Do you enjoy writing with a cup of coffee or a glass of wine within reach? Or snacking as you work? Or wearing your favorite pair of yoga pants or running shorts? Setting yourself up for a comfortable writing session can make creative work even more appealing. I love pulling on an old pair of sweats and settling in with a cup of tea to sip.

Aesthetics: What other items help you stay inspired, motivated, or focused on your writing? Do you feel most creative when you're burning a candle or surrounded by your inspiration board or other creative baubles? Do you prefer typing in a particular word processing program or writing manually with a pen and paper? Whenever possible, recreate the aesthetic circumstances that are most conducive to your personal brand of creativity. For me, bright light and digital clutter are distractions. I love working under the glow of string lights and using the Scrivener app to keep the various elements of my project in check.

Organization: Are your research notes gathered in one place? Are your various drafts and scenes neatly labeled? If you mark down a quick revision note as you write, will you know where to find it later? Developing an efficient system for organizing your work can take time, but the effort is worthwhile when your system—even if it doesn't look so organized—allows you to stay focused. I love ordering my novels' notes and scenes in Scrivener's Binder while using the Snapshots feature to track changes made between drafts.

Distractions: Have you set boundaries around your writing time so that other people won't interrupt? Have you tucked away the stack of bills or school assignments that might cause your attention to wander? Do you think of things to add to your to-do list as you write? Figure out what distracts you from your work, then make an effort to remove or reduce those distractions. I focus on completing my nonfiction priorities for the day before diving into creative writing, so I'm not tempted by an unfinished to-do list.

Clear Mental Space for Creative Work

The work you create is always more important than where and when you create it. But if you find that you write more efficiently in a specific environment or under certain conditions, make the effort to create a personal writing retreat that fulfills as many of those ideals as possible. It never hurts to set yourself up for a fantastic writing session.

That said, remember that your creative workspace is more than the location, time of day, and other physical aspects. It's also the mental space you create for your work. Many writers forget that this is just as important—if not more so—for finding the ideal conditions for your writing.

～

Activity: Clear Mental Space for Creative Work

To develop a sustainable writing practice, use the prompts on the following pages to help you claim consistent mental space for creative pursuits. Note: Some of the prompts include questions you may want to ask each time you sit down to write.

Energy: Do you have the mental and emotional energy to commit to your writing session? If you don't, what can you do instead to refill your creative well? For me, the process of reenergizing my creativity often includes taking my dog for a long walk, researching the latest historical topic that's snagged my interest, or reading a great book. (See chapter 11 for more on refilling the creative well.)

Motivation: Why are you working on this specific project? Are you passionate about the story? Will completing it help you pay the bills and keep writing? How does this project help you fulfill your personal definition of writing success? For example, I've written this book as part of my mission to create a writing business that allows me to encourage and inspire other writers. (Check out chapter 20 for more on your personal definition of writing success.)

Intention: What do you want to complete during this writing session? Do you have a specific goal in mind? What would it take to call your writing session a success? When I was working on this book, I aimed to revise two chapters per writing session. With my fiction, I prefer to work toward a time-related goal, usually just twenty or thirty minutes per day.

Permission: Are you struggling to give yourself permission to write? What limiting beliefs have convinced you that you're unworthy of making time for creative work? I often have to ignore the lie that tells me I'm not capable of overcoming difficult writing obstacles, which can lead me to question why I should bother picking up the pen.

Affirmation: If you're struggling with limiting beliefs, what words of truth can you use to reclaim your creative power? What affirmation(s) can help you clear your head of mental clutter? To uproot the limiting belief I shared in the "Permission" prompt, I frequently remind myself that, yes, I *am* capable of completing difficult creative work, and that I won't let creative turbulence define me. You can find a list of my favorite creative affirmations at the end of this book.

Limits: There's no such thing as the perfect creative space. As you set out to write, consider the physical and mental space you've defined and the limitations they present. Have you addressed these limitations as best you can? Have you set goals and intentions for your writing session that align with the limitations you've acknowledged? Though I'm most creative in the evening, I'm often too tired to write fiction after a day of working on nonfiction projects. I try to write fiction earlier in the evening, when I can still sit down with a cup of tea without worrying whether the caffeine will keep me up half the night. I also try to keep my evening writing sessions short, which helps me overcome resistance. Aiming to write for just thirty minutes every night isn't too intimidating, and I can always write for longer if I find my groove.

All things considered, life isn't always conducive to writing from the best possible headspace. But the more effort you put into adopting a healthy creative mindset, the more fluidly your writing will flow.

Using Habit Triggers

Relying on willpower alone to complete any task can be draining. This is why building a sustainable writing practice is so important. The more established your habit, the less you'll need to draw upon willpower to get started. This will make it easier to circumvent resistance and keep writing. That said, you can make building and maintaining that practice even easier by taking, quite literally, the path of least resistance—by finding ways to rely less on willpower and more on habit each time you set out to write.

To do so, consider creating a habit trigger, an action you'd perform exclusively before or during a habit you're looking to solidify or maintain. James Clear, author of *Atomic Habits*, calls this practice "habit stacking" and encourages building a new practice on top of a well-established daily habit, such as getting dressed in the morning or eating your evening snack. Here are a few examples of habit triggers you might want to employ to build and sustain your writing practice:

- After I make my morning cup of coffee, I will write for twenty minutes.
- As I eat lunch, I will plan out the scene I want to write when I get home.
- After dinner, I will send my daily email to my critique partner.
- After tucking my kids into bed, I will spend thirty minutes researching and querying agents.

You can compound the power of a habit trigger by stacking several easy habits that lead to the new habit you're developing. For example, to build and solidify your evening writing routine, you might make a cup of tea to drink as you write immediately after finishing dinner. You can strengthen the power of this routine by choosing one tea to drink exclusively during your writing sessions. Doing so will forge a neural link between your favorite beverage and your creative work, further helping you circumvent resistance.

Habit triggers can help you develop your ideal creative headspace—and in some cases, your physical workspace as well. You might want to clear your desk before each writing session, light a fragrant candle, or readjust your inspiration board. These actions, which we discussed earlier in this chapter, are just as much habit triggers as any other.

Defining the ritual that best helps you claim your creative space might be challenging. Habit triggers are highly personal and often arbitrary, but it's important to choose habit triggers that align with your ideal physical workspace and creative headspace. Don't be afraid to explore several potential triggers that interest you. If you often have to fit writing into the margins of your life, you might want to create several sets of triggers to encourage work under different circumstances.

When it comes to circumventing resistance, consistency is a powerful weapon, but so is flexibility. Your ideal writing conditions will likely evolve over time, and that's okay. They might even vary depending on the project you're pursuing or your current stage in the writing process. Feel free to make changes to your workspace if any aspect no longer serves your habit. As long as you practice flexibility, you can create a personal writing retreat, clear your mind for creative work, and harness the power of habit triggers—all of which can help you build a writing life you love.

9

ROCKING YOUR WRITING PROCESS

I think there are two types of writers, the architects and the gardeners. The architects plan everything ahead of time, like an architect building a house. . . . The gardeners dig a hole, drop in a seed, and water it.

—George R. R. Martin,
best-selling author of *A Game of Thrones* and
other books in the Song of Ice and Fire series

Every writer's process is unique. How I approach my writing might not work as well for you, and that's perfectly fine. Your job is to explore different methods and techniques and determine which align with your creative preferences. If you're unhappy with your current writing process or can't say for sure that you have one, now's the time to discover how you work best. Let's start with five common areas where subtle differences make each writer's process unique and personally effective.

Common Area: Tools

Most writers work electronically, using word processors such as Microsoft Word, Google Docs, or Scrivener. If you're one of these writers, which program do you prefer to use? Consider the functionality of each processor and the features that would help you create your best work.

Some writers, however, stick to a manual process, using pen and paper instead of typing. If this is your preferred writing mode, give some thought to the materials you use. What size notebook fits your needs best? Which type of writing utensil do you prefer?

Maybe you enjoy using certain tools at different stages of your writing process. For example, some writers prefer to draft their stories by hand and then type their work. Other writers love drafting in a simple computer program that's free of distracting features before transferring their work to Scrivener and using the app's editing tools. Still others enjoy dictating their first drafts or recording notes as voice memos that they later revise or copy into their favorite word processor.

Personally, I prefer to write and revise in Scrivener, which is designed specifically for long-form content such as novels, nonfiction books, and dissertations. I often use Scrivener for Mac's dictation feature as I draft as well, especially for nonfiction projects such as this book.

Also, don't forget to consider which tools you'll use to back up your work. Losing thousands of words to a failed save, computer crash, or notebook dropped in the mud can be devastating. To avoid this, use a backup system that doesn't involve emailing your manuscript to yourself or manually uploading your work to cloud storage—preferably a system that works automatically. For example, I like to house my projects in the Dropbox folder on my computer. Every time Scrivener saves (which happens after every two-second typing pause), Dropbox automatically uploads the newest version of the document to my free Dropbox cloud account.

Common Area: Organization

The writing life often results in endless computer files and scribbled notes. If you don't have a physical or digital system in place to organize these items, consider how this might be detrimental to your writing process.

Before I discovered Scrivener, I saved each chapter of a writing project as an individual Microsoft Word file. Drafting an entire project in one document seemed inefficient, given that I liked to refer to previously written chapters and view several of them at once. Yet organizing all of my chapter files and readjusting program windows to view multiple documents proved inefficient as well. And that was in addition to the journals full of character and world-building notes I kept hidden in a desk drawer.

Creating an organization system using Scrivener has since made my writing life less messy and frustrating. The app allows me to create and house multiple folders, subfolders, and documents within a single project file via a feature called the Binder. It also lets me view multiple documents within a file at once, as well as old versions of each chapter using the Snapshot feature. (For more information on how I use Scrivener, visit well-storied.com/scrivener-tutorials.)

Your own organization system might differ. Maybe you have no problem drafting a project in a single Word file while keeping project notes in a color-coded three-ring binder. Or maybe you file your handwritten drafts by date and maintain strict computer folders for organizing digital documents. So long as your method allows for efficient work, it's the right method for you.

Common Area: Prewriting

Prewriting is the process of preparing to draft a story. It's the work that comes before the actual writing and helps writers prepare for a successful first draft. Common prewriting tasks include researching, outlining, crafting characters, defining a story's setting and theme, and developing a fictional world.

Prewriting is perhaps the area in which writers' processes differ the most, so much so that some writers have adopted labels that identify whether they enjoy prewriting. *Pantsers* are writers who don't find prewriting beneficial to their process. Instead, they "write by the seat of their pants," exploring their characters and plots as they draft. This process is sometimes called "discovery drafting." *Plotters*, on the other hand, thrive when they take the time to develop their stories before writing. They don't have to complete a set amount of prewriting to call themselves a plotter, but generally, the term implies that the writer knows a good deal about their story before they write it. Finally, *plantsers* are writers whose prewriting process combines elements of pantsing and plotting. They typically complete light prewriting work, defining the most important hallmarks of their characters and plots before developing the details as they draft.

Personally, I'm a plotter—a very extreme plotter. I fully develop my characters, plots, themes, and fictional worlds using the many methods I outline on my website. Developing my story in as much detail as possible before writing allows me to move quickly through the first draft, which is my least favorite part of the writing process.

Regardless of where you fall on the plotting-or-pantsing spectrum, consider which tools, structures, and techniques help you complete your best prewriting work. Do you use the Hero's Journey, Snowflake Method, Three-Act Story Structure, or Story Grid to outline your story's plot? Do you develop your characters by answering a specific questionnaire, journaling from their perspectives, or using a personality test such as the Enneagram of Personality or Myers–Briggs Type Indicator?

You can find myriad resources to help you through each stage of the prewriting process, from characterization and outlining to research and world-building. Take time to explore some of these resources for yourself. Again, I share many of my own techniques and favorite resources on the Well-Storied blog.

Common Area: Drafting

While the term *draft* refers to any completed, unpublished version of your project, the term *drafting* specifically refers to the process of writing the first draft. What your personal writing process looks like while drafting can vary.

Some writers prefer to write what's called a *skeleton draft* or a *draft zero*, a quick version of their story that gets the bare bones of each scene onto the page. A passage from a skeleton draft might look like this:

> The moon is shining through the window in the library. Mary is standing before the fire, a glass of brandy in her hand, when Thomas comes in.
>> I always knew you were a liar. —Mary
> Thomas knows she's discovered his secret, but he pretends ignorance.
>> I'm sorry? —Thomas
>> You ought to be. —M
>> I don't know what you mean, darling. —T
>> Stop that. Stop pretending I'm a fool! —M
> In a rage, M throws the glass of brandy at T's head.

A skeleton draft is a great option for pantsers and plantsers, since it allows them to explore scenes they might cut without spending precious writing time on a complete draft. Plotters, on the other hand, generally don't benefit from skeleton drafts. Because they develop their outlines and refine their plots prior to drafting, their stories are less likely to need heavy rewrites. Therefore, it makes sense for plotters to draft in full—though some plotters do write skeleton drafts as a form of extreme outlining rather than part of their drafting process.

The speed at which writers draft can also vary greatly. This isn't solely based on the amount of time they have to write, though. Some writers complete what's called a *fast draft* in which they get their stories down as quickly as possible, then put more time into meticulous revisions. Other writers call themselves *turtle writers*; they complete slow but steady first drafts that allow them to produce cleaner versions of their manuscripts.

Personally, I write my first drafts in full, since I've already taken the time to develop them during prewriting. And since I don't enjoy the drafting process, I fast-draft my stories so I can move more quickly into the part of the writing process I enjoy best: revising.

Common Area: Revising and Editing

The terms *revising* and *editing* are often used interchangeably. However, *revision* refers to story-level changes, while *editing* concerns the prose, or the language of the story. Typically, a writer revises before they edit, as polishing prose matters little if the scene is destined to find itself on the cutting room floor.

When exploring how you best complete both of these processes, consider whether revising and editing energize you. If you don't enjoy them as I do, you'll likely want to cut down on the time you need to spend revising and editing by prewriting your stories and crafting as clean a first draft as possible. However, if they do energize you, you might want to fast-draft your work or complete a skeleton draft so you can save your energy for these later stages.

The biggest difference between how writers revise and how they edit is the type of work they do in each draft and, therefore, how many drafts they complete. To avoid overwhelm, some writers prefer to revise and edit in many small drafts, tackling just one or two concerns at a time (e.g., revising first to fix plot inconsistencies, then again to focus on character development, then again to improve dialogue). Other writers prefer to tackle revising and editing in several large passes, completing any necessary work on each chapter and scene.

When exploring your own revising and editing processes, you might also want to consider if and when you'll seek feedback from beta readers, critique partners, or an editor. More on this topic is coming in chapter 19 of this book.

Personally, I prefer to invest the bulk of my time and energy in revising and editing, completing expansive drafts that tackle many story issues at once. I also seek feedback only when I have a strong draft of the project ready.

Develop Your Personal Writing Process

Developing your writing process is much like buying a new car. Based on your needs, preferences, and past experiences, you head to the dealership with an understanding of the vehicle you believe will serve you best. Test-driving that vehicle will likely confirm your beliefs. This same principle applies to your writing process.

Certain writing techniques will pique your interest because they align with your natural tendencies. If you love technology and tools designed to improve your performance, you might enjoy using Scrivener or other advanced writing apps. If you're prone to overwhelm, you might want to revise in several small drafts to avoid incorporating all of your desired changes at once. And if you tend to rebel against rules and expectations, you might not want to prewrite your work, since you'll likely diverge from your outline the second you get the chance.

But what if you pull up to the car dealership knowing exactly what you want, only to discover that the car isn't the right option for you? Or if you don't have the slightest clue as to which car will serve your needs best? In either case, a series of test-drives is your best plan of action.

When considering your writing process, don't be afraid to explore new techniques. Go ahead and try a skeleton draft if the idea intrigues you. If you later realize that it doesn't allow you to connect well with your story, you can switch to writing your scenes in full. Consider testing a major rewrite. If find yourself bogged down by doubts about your revision skills, you can step back and focus on one issue at a time instead. How about if you're trying a new word processor but its features are too complex and distracting? You can always return to a simpler option.

At some point in your writing life, you might find a part of your writing process no longer works for you. In this situation, you have two options: add to the resistance you're facing by refusing to make changes, or start exploring a new method that will help you rock your writing process again. Doing so may take time and patience, but that effort will prove worthwhile when you discover the tool or technique that enables you to continue creating your best work.

~

Activity: Develop Your Personal Writing Process

Using a sheet of paper, draw three columns and label them "To Incorporate," "To Explore," and "To Reevaluate." Then, review each of the five common areas of a writer's process that were covered in this chapter. See which methods and techniques catch your eye, and sort them into each column as follows:

Under "To Incorporate," list any techniques you believe fit well into your writing process based on your natural tendencies. These are the techniques you'll immediately incorporate into your writing process. Under "To Explore," list any techniques you want to explore but aren't sure will work well for your process. Under "To Reevaluate," list any techniques that you've tried or are currently part of your process but don't serve your needs anymore.

Once you've finished, plan to revisit the techniques listed under "To Explore" and "To Reevaluate" as needed.

～

10

IMPROVING YOUR WRITING OUTPUT

Show up. Put in the work. Let go of the outcome.

—Victoria "V. E." Schwab,
best-selling author of fantasy fiction

E fficiency has recently been a hot topic in the writing community. With the advent of digital self-publishing, authors have had to rely on frequent releases to build and maintain their readerships in a constantly flooded market. Having an accomplished backlist of books (i.e., a list of older books still in print) also helps modern writers build credibility with readers without the backing of a publishing house. Therefore, the more books a writer publishes, the more likely they are to maintain a stable and successful career.

It's no wonder writers are now asking how they can increase their writing output. Even those who aren't interested in publishing for profit are feeling pressured to increase their productivity to prove that they're in some way "real" writers.

But in truth, "productivity" is a dangerous buzzword I would love to banish from every writer's repertoire.

Productivity itself is measured as the rate of output per unit of input. As a writer, your input is time and your output is word count. Your productivity as a writer is therefore determined by how many words you can write or revise in as little time as possible. But here's the thing: writers shouldn't feel compelled to treat themselves like machines driven by their craft.

The Trouble with Seeking Productivity in Your Writing Life

Measuring productivity might work well for factory owners seeking to increase profits, but creative output isn't so clinically consistent. Writing the death of a character's loved one, for example, will likely be more difficult than crafting witty banter. Yet both of these elements might be vital to your story. Why, then, would the hour you spent writing five hundred solemn words prove less productive than the fifteen minutes you spent on the same amount of sassy dialogue?

At the end of the day, fifteen minutes is fifteen minutes, regardless of whether you're writing with a headache or after a good night's sleep. You might produce more in the same amount of time when you're feeling well, but if you put in the time and the best effort you have to offer, are you less productive when your word count isn't as numerically great? Technically, yes.

Productivity preaches that your best effort isn't good enough on some days because you didn't produce as much work as you did the day before. This is why striving for productivity can prove so problematic for writers. The more you seek to measure your writerly self-worth by the number of words you write or revise on any given day, the more shame you'll feel as your creative output ebbs and flows.

Resistance loves nothing more than to stoke feelings of

inadequacy. "See?" it says. "You didn't match yesterday's word count. At this rate, you'll never finish your book." Don't give resistance another crack to slip through. Instead of working to increase your productivity, reframe the way you measure your everyday writing progress.

The Most Effective Way to Measure Your Creative Output

Remember the quote by Victoria "V. E." Schwab at the beginning of this chapter? Her simple mantra revolutionized the way I viewed my creative output. For years, I'd been heeding authors who swore the key to their success lay in writing at least one thousand words per day. I wanted their success. But no matter how hard I worked, I just couldn't consistently reach the daily word count they claimed to produce. I felt like a failure.

Seeing Schwab, one of my favorite authors, proclaim that she measures her creative output by letting go of arbitrary goals and instead honoring the time and effort she puts in turned my world upside down in the best way possible.

Some writers might find it beneficial to work to a daily word count, especially if they write full-time or work to a small daily minimum. (For example, one of my previous writing routines involved writing a minimum of two hundred words each day, which often took me as little as ten minutes to achieve.) But this might not be the best way for writers who are frustrated with their current creative output to effectively measure their progress.

Are you putting in the time and effort? Then what more can you ask? You're giving your writing all you have to give, and that's more than good enough. So let go of the outcome. All progress is good progress, regardless of the circumstances, and your input will likely take you further than you'd expect.

Consider John Grisham's early writing life. Grisham was a

new father and practicing attorney when he wrote his debut novel, *A Time to Kill*. Now he's an international best-seller. How did he make it happen? By committing himself to just one written page per day, a goal he found achievable enough to push through the resistance to wait until he had more time to write. Sometimes he wrote more than one page, and sometimes he didn't. But it wasn't his output that mattered. By making the consistent effort to write one page per day, Grisham achieved his goal of writing a book and much, much more.

Do You Want to Improve Your Creative Output?

There's nothing wrong with wanting to be a more efficient writer so long as your motivation stems from the desire to overcome challenges in your writing life. Personally, I'm working toward reducing the amount of time I spend self-editing as I draft. For me, self-editing so early in the writing process indicates the pull of perfectionism, which is why I'm tackling this issue with intention.

~

Activity: Improve Your Writing Output

If you're dissatisfied with your writing output, then answer the following questions:

- In what way am I dissatisfied with my writing output?
- Why am I dissatisfied with this effort?
- What deeper issue does this dissatisfaction reveal?
- How would I like to increase my output?
- Why do I want to increase my output in this way?

Be specific in your answers. The deeper you dig, the more insight you'll gain into whether increasing your writing output is truly a beneficial goal for your writing practice.

By answering these questions, you'll likely find that the root of your dissatisfaction lies in a matter of skill or mindset, both of which are within your control. For example, if you're dissatisfied with the rate at which you're revising, this might be a result of not knowing how to objectively evaluate your plot arcs or character development. These skills can be studied and improved upon; this and other topics pertaining to the improvement of your writing skills will be covered in part 3 of this book.

But contrary to matters of skill, the reason I struggle with making unnecessary edits stems from a matter of mindset. For many writers, this common distraction during the drafting process is a form of perfectionism—which, as we discussed in chapter 4, results from a fear of criticism. And the only way to overcome fear is to choose bravery and take effective action. That's why I used affirmations and a self-imposed deadline to curtail my perfectionism as I drafted this book.

If you're dissatisfied with your creative output, take a good look at the source of your dissatisfaction. Will working toward improving your productivity help you overcome a specific challenge in your writing life, or is it merely an arbitrary goal?

If you can identify such a challenge, then do your best to resolve it. The steps you take will be unique to your situation, and throughout this book, you can find ideas on how to move forward. Don't hesitate to set aside your current writing goal if you need to. One small backward step now can prevent a major misstep down the road; once you discover how to increase your writing output, you'll more than make up for any time you've spent away from your work.

Finally, remember that all progress is good progress. Harness the time you have to write, and put in the best effort you have to offer. Do this on a consistent basis, and you'll build a writing practice that makes your best writing life a reality.

11

REFILLING THE CREATIVE WELL

As artists, we must learn to be self-nourishing. We must become alert enough to consciously replenish our creative resources as we draw on them—to restock the trout pond, so to speak. I call this process filling the well.

—Julia Cameron,
The Artist's Way

Inside every writer sits a creative well. Whenever you sit down to write, you dip your bucket into this well, drawing the energy you need to attend the work at hand.

The energy in your creative well is a renewable resource, but the rate at which it renews depends on many factors. When surrounded by sources of inspiration, your well overflows, leading you to create at a frenzied pace. But when life becomes stressful, your creative well fills more slowly, with much of its energy diverted to other priorities. On most days, however, a writer's creative well renews at a rate somewhere between the two extremes.

Draw one small bucket or two each time you sit down to write, and your well will refill steadily enough to allow you to sustain your writing practice. But if you draw too deeply and too often from your well, you can use up all the energy you've been storing. This state is often called *writing burnout*, a complete creative exhaustion that leaves you too weary to do what you love. You might experience this when working to meet a deadline, striving to maintain your writing routine during a difficult period of life, or chasing a self-imposed goal or standard. This additional stress quickly drains you of your creative energy until your well runs dry.

Waiting around for your creative well to refill can be frustrating. Fortunately, you can take certain steps to mindfully accelerate this process—and better yet, to honor periods of low energy so you can prevent writing burnout in the first place. The next time you sit down to write, check in with yourself. How full is your creative well? The signs are often obvious. If you're full of inspiration, your well might be overflowing with a flood of new ideas. Get to work, then, and bear in mind that inspiration often recedes as quickly as it arrives. If you're not feeling overly inspired but are ready to work nonetheless, you've likely built a sustainable writing practice in which you draw from your creative well with care. Well done!

But what if you simply don't want to write? This could be a sign that your creative well is running low. Determining what to do next, however, can be tricky. Resistance loves to disempower you by zapping your creative energy before you pick up the pen. It does this by preying upon your doubts and fears, convincing you that you aren't good enough to do the work you've been meaning to do.

In this case, taking a break to refill your creative well isn't the answer. You have the energy to write. Resistance has simply stopped up your well to convince you otherwise. To tap into your hidden creative energy, you'll need to dig deep into your limiting beliefs and take action to overcome your fear. Often, this means putting in the damn hard work that is writing.

But if you've been drawing too much from your creative energy over a short period of time, chances are you're experiencing a legitimate case of writing burnout. Your well is dry. You have little to give to your stories. It's time to refill.

How to Refill Your Creative Well

When you write, you expend creative energy. Therefore, the easiest way to refill your well is to consume more of this energy. What have others created that you can enjoy or digest? Any form of creation counts, such as films, music, poetry, or art.

As a writer, your most obvious source of creative consumption is reading. You come to know your craft most intimately when you consume the works of other writers. Therefore, one of the primary ways you become a better writer is by reading. This is something I'll explain further in part 3 of this book.

But weren't you a reader before you became a writer? Didn't the stories you've consumed inspire you to write stories of your own? If you aren't already making time to read, I encourage you to do so. It's by far one of the best ways to refill your creative well. That said, don't discount the power in consuming other kinds of creativity. Any form of art or innovation counts. If someone has created it, it has the power to recreate you.

Activity: Source Water for the Well

List the ways in which you can consume creative energy. Be as specific as possible. Is there a book you've been itching to read? A television show you'd love to binge? A local art museum you've wanted to visit? Consider how to make time to enjoy some of these sources of inspiration on a regular basis or as a special occasion. Julia Cameron, author of *The Artist's Way*, calls the latter activity an "artist's date" and recommends taking yourself on such a date once a week.

Consuming the work of others is a fantastic way to revive your creative energy, but it's not the only approach you can take. Here are a few other methods you can try:

Mind Your Priorities

Writing will always drain you if you're using it as a way to procrastinate in other important areas of life. Take time to review the list of priorities you created in chapter 7. Which ones do you need to attend now so you can write with a clear head and conscience?

Meditate on Your Mindset

Honing a healthy creative mindset is a project in and of itself. Are you facing new challenges in your writing life that might wear you down over time? What weak points in your mindset might resistance try to exploit? Continue to address these issues so you can reclaim the energy resistance is draining from your well.

Go Outside

Research shows that spending time in nature has a restorative effect on your physical and mental well-being. To refill your creative well, consider taking a long walk in the countryside, going on a day hike, or spending time at the beach. You can even garden or sunbathe to gain this same restorative effect. If you live in an urban area, what local parks or zoos do you have access to? Or can you escape the city for a day? No matter your preferred activity, getting outside can provide fresh inspiration and respite from creative overload.

Get Involved in the Writing Community

Writing is often solitary work. It's easy to think you're alone in the struggles that drain your creative energy. But by interacting with other writers, you'll find creative kinship in sharing your common challenges, discovering new solutions to old problems, and stirring up a healthy dose of inspiration to refill your well.

Engage in Other Creative Activities

Do you enjoy drawing, painting, or creating other visual art? Do you sing or play musical instruments? Are you a cook, baker, or dancer? Even if you don't have the energy to write, taking up activities that involve a different brand of creativity can stimulate your brain and recharge you for your next writing session.

Make Room for a Little R&R

Whether it's for a month, a week, or even an evening, taking a break from your writing might make you feel as though you're failing to maintain your writing practice. But you can't create your best work if you don't have energy to give. Watching a movie marathon, lounging by the pool, taking a nap, and getting coffee with a friend are fantastic ways to renew yourself when you burn out—no guilt or shame necessary.

How to Recuperate from Writing Burnout

Think you might be dealing with a case of writing burnout? Don't let resistance shame you for overdrawing from your creative well. Instead, take a step back. Set your creative projects aside for a few days (or weeks), and spend time refilling your creative well using some of the tips shared in this chapter.

Recuperating from writing burnout is a surprisingly simple process, but it does take time. Be patient. You'll know you're ready to write again when you find yourself eager to return to your stories—or when resistance insists you aren't ready. Acknowledge that negative self-talk, recognize it for what it is, then tap into your creative well and write.

12

WORKING THROUGH WRITER'S BLOCK

There's no such thing as writer's block. That was invented by people in California who couldn't write.

—Terry Pratchett,
best-selling author of the
Discworld series and *Good Omens*

You want to write, but you're blocked. An insurmountable obstacle stands between you and your manuscript, and you're frustrated. Beyond frustrated. What is writer's block, anyway? Why can't you seem to kick it to the curb, no matter how much you want to get back to work? The truth of the matter is that you're kicking empty air.

That's right. Writer's block isn't a real creative obstacle, at least in the context of how most writers define this term. The muse hasn't departed. You aren't doomed. You've simply taken a wrong turn in your writing journey. As David H. Safford wrote in an article for The Write Practice, "[Writer's block is] the self-inflicted phenomenon of writers making choices that frequently lead to failure." In other words, it isn't a condition, but rather a decision you make to avoid responsibility for failing to address resistance in your writing life. Oof!

This reality can be a tough pill to swallow. But the sooner you take responsibility for your creative missteps, the sooner you can take action to resolve them.

Though writer's block doesn't exist as most writers define it, I'll continue referring to it as "writer's block" for the remainder of this chapter for ease of use. With that established, what steps can you take to reclaim responsibility for your writing life and claw your way out of the grip of resistance?

The Reality of Writer's Block

Writer's block can be a tough topic to tackle because each instance is unique. It's an umbrella term for any deep struggle with limiting beliefs that results from a variety of issues writers commonly face during their journey. But at its core, one thread weaves through every case of writer's block: a negative reaction to doubt.

Remember that doubt is not your creative enemy. It simply represents an area of uncertainty in your writing life. It's a question that needs answering, a prompt that demands action. But taking action in the face of uncertainty can be difficult. Resistance knows this, and it will try to twist doubt into the limiting belief that you are incapable or unworthy. It's when you accept this belief with open arms that you run into writer's block.

The key to overcoming writer's block lies in confronting your doubts and moving forward. But to do so, you'll need to dig deep into the source of these doubts. Let's look at the four most common causes in this chapter.

Cause 1: You Aren't Taking Care of Your Creative Mindset

Maintaining a healthy creative mindset is an ongoing experience. Each phase of your writing life will introduce new challenges that can lead to doubts you haven't experienced before or renew old ones. If you don't mind your headspace, resistance will worm its way through the first crack it can find to sow a new set of limiting beliefs. And then it won't be long before your struggle with fear, perfectionism, or other negative patterns leads to a nasty case of writer's block.

Cause 2: You've Encountered Overwhelming Craft-Related Issues

Writing a compelling and cohesive book is no easy task. The work that's needed to resolve craft-related issues can often be overwhelming, leading you to question whether you're capable of making the necessary changes. Many writers who encounter this doubt respond by shutting down or overthinking—and walk themselves straight into writer's block.

Cause 3: You're Experiencing Writing Burnout

You have a limited supply of creative energy, and if you've pushed yourself beyond your limits as a writer, you've likely burned yourself out. When this happens, you don't have the energy needed to confront resistance, let alone write. This is when writer's block sets in.

Cause 4: You Haven't Been Flexible with Your Writing Life

Establishing your personal writing practice, process, and creative space are all fantastic ways to build consistency into your writing life, circumvent resistance, and set yourself up for success. But as you grow and evolve as a writer, and as your schedule and environment change over time, each of these elements must evolve with you. If you fail to change your practice or process as the rest of your life changes, you'll risk falling victim to writer's block.

Take Action Against Writer's Block

Uncertainty will remain a regular part of your writing life. That much *is* certain. But if you don't confront that uncertainty, you'll find yourself stumbling into writer's block over and over again. The key to clawing your way out lies in taking action. Just as waiting for the muse to inspire you won't help you finish a manuscript, waiting for writer's block to pass on its own won't help you overcome it.

∾

Activity: Kick Writer's Block to the Curb

To dig deep into the heart of your writer's block, ask yourself these questions:

- What circumstances led me to embrace resistance?
- In what way(s) do I feel incapable or unworthy?

When you can answer these questions honestly and in detail, you can take the necessary steps to counteract your unique experience with writer's block. Refer to related chapters throughout this book—such as 2, 9, 11, and 15—for further guidance.

∾

Is your writer's block a result of plot issues that you fear you can't resolve? Go back to the source. Study common plot structures and techniques, then create a list of step-by-step actions you can take to untangle the issues in your story. Remember that you're as good a writer as you work toward being.

Did you burn through your creative energy in an attempt to meet a self-imposed deadline? Take a break from your manuscript, and spend time refilling your creative well. If stepping back leads to feelings of guilt or shame, remember that you are not your writing output. You can't complete your best work if you're working yourself into the ground.

Lastly, know that low points will be as common in your writing journey as the highs. Despite this, creative turbulence doesn't define you. Your commitment to your craft does. There will always be times when writing will be difficult, your process will need refining, or your mindset will need shoring up. Like doubts, these moments are not the enemy. They're opportunities.

Take action so you can consistently work toward becoming the writer you want to be. Your best writing life isn't waiting over the horizon. It's here. It's now. Give yourself time and grace, and you'll learn to navigate creative lows as confidently as every other step in your writing journey.

13

BUILDING WRITING ENDURANCE

Exerting yourself to the fullest within your individual limits: that's the essence of running, and a metaphor for life—and for me, for writing as well.

—Haruki Murakami,
What I Talk About When I Talk About Running

Building a successful writing practice isn't about working harder or faster than those around you. Writing isn't a competition, and neither is publishing. Rather, writing is a marathon of the mind.

Just as runners with different body types and distance goals must adopt unique training techniques to achieve peak performance, you must develop a writing practice that best fits your creative build if you want to hit your writing stride.

Hopefully, the past eight chapters have helped you do just that. With your new writing practice in place, you might be wondering how to maintain this practice for the long haul and build the endurance you need to achieve your personal definition of writing success. We'll break down how you can define success for yourself in part 4 of this book. But for now, let's continue looking at the concept of writing endurance through the eyes of a runner.

When marathon runners train, they seek to improve on distance and speed. As a result, they also improve on endurance and overall athletic performance. Writers pursuing their marathons of the mind can find similar benefits in creative training. But what exactly does that training look like? And how does it lead to writing endurance *and* improvement in your creative performance?

How to Increase Your Writing Distance

For writers, distance can be found in a creative practice they can maintain for years to come. The best way to maintain this practice is through slow and steady consistency. A runner who trains only occasionally or pushes their body to the point of injury is unlikely to get very far. By working to create at a measured and mindful pace, you'll outdistance any writer who relies on mad-dash work sessions and spurts of inspiration to drive them to the page.

In addition, consistency demands balance. Physical training isn't always easy, and neither is writing. You'll need to learn when it's best to push through resistance and write and when you've begun to push yourself past your limits. Again, be mindful of your creative energy. It's better to skip a day of writing to refill your creative well than it is to miss a week because you ran yourself into writing burnout.

Finding the consistency and balance you need to go the distance in your writing life can be tricky, but remember that endurance is built with time. Be patient with yourself, especially when you're first developing your writing practice. You're going to experience growing pains, and resistance will double down when it sees the effort you're putting into building your best writing life.

Keep moving forward, and forgive yourself when you slip up. It's not creative turbulence that defines you, but rather your commitment to your craft. Get back on your feet, and allow your missteps to guide you as you learn to pace yourself. The steadier your efforts, the further you'll fly.

~

Activity: Pace Your Writing Progress

To maintain your writing practice for the long haul, set the following three goals for writing sessions:

- **Maintenance Goal:** This is a goal you can achieve on a typical day in your writing practice. For me, this goal is thirty minutes of writing or revising fiction each evening.
- **Stretch Goal:** This second goal challenges you to increase your endurance when you have the time and energy to spare. My stretch goal is one hour of work on my fiction.
- **Recovery Goal:** This final goal is one you can achieve on days when you're recovering from burnout or when life has thrown a wrench into your writing practice. Ten minutes of writing or revising generally works well for my recovery goal.

Each time you sit down for a writing session, choose the goal that best fits the amount of creative energy you have to give to your work on that particular day. Remember to remain flexible, and adjust your goals as necessary when switching between projects or different parts of the writing process.

~

How to Increase Your Writing Speed

In chapter 10, we covered measuring your writing progress by the time and effort you put in rather than the output you produce, including why it can be problematic to seek increased productivity. Why, then, are we discussing how you can increase your writing speed? In this case, speed isn't how much you're able to write in as little time as possible. Rather, it's an increase in focused effort that sees you moving more quickly toward the next milestone in your writing journey.

Heaven knows we writers love to dawdle; as I'll share in chapter 20, there are times when dawdling can actually prove productive. But how often have you stared at the blinking cursor on your screen, puzzling over what to write next? Or reviewed a chapter just one more time instead of moving forward? Or fallen victim to procrastination instead of getting started?

These are some of the ways writers dawdle in their creative work, and you must confront these recurring instances to increase the pace of your writing. Dawdling often results from a tangle with resistance, so check in with your creative mindset regularly. What lingering limiting beliefs can you uproot? How can you take action in the face of doubt or fear?

The Power of Tracking Your Progress

It's easy to lose sight of how much you've accomplished when you're working toward a long-term goal. This is why I encourage writers to track their progress. In doing so, you'll map the evidence of your efforts and accomplishments, which you can review any time you're feeling down. This practice can then help you build confidence in your creative potential and abilities.

~

Activity: Track Your Writing Progress

First, decide what you'd like to track: the time you put in, your daily word count, your progress toward specific goals or milestones, or all of the above.

Then, make note of your progress after each writing session. You can do this by creating a spreadsheet, making a list in your journal, using the accomplishments tracker in the back of the Novel Planner (which you can access at well-storied.com/the-novel-planner), or adopting any other method that suits your fancy. This simple task takes only seconds to complete, yet its insights can prove incredibly encouraging as you build endurance and increase your writing speed.

~

In addition to tracking your progress, you might also want to consider some of the following tips for developing writing endurance.

Establish a Strong Why

If you don't want to run a marathon, you won't likely endure the training process, let alone find fulfillment in crossing the finish line. Strong motivations, however, transform demanding tasks into fulfilling challenges. So why do you want to write?

Do you want to pen the stories you've longed to read? Is writing your emotional outlet or an escape from the daily grind? Do you want to educate or inspire others? Are you writing a tale to share with your children or grandchildren?

Set Goals and Make a Plan

Setting short-term goals can help you maintain focus and endurance as you build your best writing life. To set effective goals, first identify a milestone achievement that would help you turn your writing dreams into reality. Do you want to finish your manuscript? Land an agent? Self-publish your next book? Then, identify the small steps you can take to reach that milestone. Use this plan to guide and motivate you in your everyday writing life. We'll talk more about charting your personal road map to writing success in part 4 of this book.

Hold Yourself Accountable

With a strong work ethic and clear motivation, you shouldn't have any trouble holding yourself accountable to your writing practice. But if, like me, you thrive on external accountability and validation, then seek it out. Participate in the online writing community. Join an in-person writing group. Find critique partners, beta readers, an editor, or a writing coach with whom you genuinely connect. Knowing that others are expecting and encouraging you to succeed can provide the healthy pressure you need to make those goals a reality.

Celebrate Often

Building writing endurance is hard work; don't hesitate to celebrate your gains. Whether you've reached a particular word count, completed a new draft of your project, or just had a good writing day, take time to honor that accomplishment—and don't forget to track it. Celebrating can be as simple as sharing your joy with a friend or fellow writer or as elaborate as a special meal or travel experience to mark the occasion. Do whatever feels most rewarding to you.

Seek Growth

Finally, remember that you can't become a better writer by stagnating in your training. Just as runners seek to improve performance, writers should work with intention to improve their skills and tell better stories. If you aren't sure how to get started, have no fear. Part 3 of this book will share everything you need to know about seeking intentional growth.

PART III

TOOLS FOR INTENTIONAL GROWTH

Intention:
  : a determination to act in a certain way; resolve
  : what one intends to do or bring about

—Merriam-Webster

The universe doesn't give you what you ask for with your thoughts—it gives you what you demand with your actions.

—Steve Maraboli,
Life, the Truth, and Being Free

14

THE POWER IN SEEKING INTENTIONAL GROWTH

We have to continually be jumping off cliffs and developing our wings on the way down.

—Kurt Vonnegut,
American author and playwright

You're as good a writer as you work toward being. This is a truth I first established in chapter 2. If you have a passion for stories and want to improve your ability to tell them, you can do exactly that. Forget about talent. It might be a boon to creative endeavors, but it isn't essential to producing quality work. All that's required is that you take 100 percent responsibility for your growth. If you're willing to put in the time and effort to seek self-improvement, you can become the writer you want to be.

Already, you've taken the first step in this journey by building a sustainable writing practice. The more you write, the more you'll develop your writing skills, even if you aren't actively focusing on any specific ability. This development might not be readily apparent, but hindsight is twenty-twenty. Compare a piece of work you wrote six months ago to a piece from last week, and you'll realize how much you've grown. It's an exciting revelation. But the improvement that results from your writing practice is passive. It doesn't reflect your full ability as a writer.

To take an active role in developing your writing and story-telling skills, seek intentional growth. Get clear about where and how you'd like to improve in your writing life, and take the necessary steps to manifest that improvement. In the following chapters, I'll share four strategies for seeking growth in your writing life. But you can't put those strategies to work if you don't know why you'd like to employ them. To identify areas of potential growth as a writer, you must first discover your personal writing strengths and weaknesses.

Identify Your Writing Strengths and Weaknesses

Writers frequently find themselves drawn to the blank page by a love of story, a love of language, or both. In my experience, these interests indicate a writer's natural strengths in the craft —and reveal their weaknesses. This certainly holds true in my own experience.

I've always been a voracious reader and daydreamer. But while I dabbled in writing stories when I was younger, I didn't embrace the writing life until my final year of high school. Desperate to pass time as I awaited graduation day, I dreamed up a story idea so captivating that I continued writing long after donning my cap and gown. My creative strengths became apparent in the months that followed. I'd happily spend endless hours creating characters and developing story lines. But when it came time to translate that story onto the page, each word felt like pulling teeth. I simply had no natural knack for writing prose.

If this struggle resonates with you, your writing strengths likely lie in storytelling. But if it doesn't, your strengths might be in language instead. Perhaps you excel at composing stunning lyrical prose but can't seem to develop a story idea you're excited to explore. Or maybe you love writing snippets of exciting scenes but have trouble developing full-length stories. Does either scenario sound familiar? Occasionally, a writer will have a natural flair for both of these elements. These writers are often immensely talented, but there's no need to worry if you aren't one of them. Every writer, regardless of their creative aptitude, will encounter areas of their ability that need improvement—and these aren't necessarily weak points in their craft.

If you're new to writing or haven't yet developed a healthy creative mindset, you might assume you have no strengths as a writer. This couldn't be further from the truth. What defines a strength isn't knowledge or developed skill. It's *energy*. Passion. An excitement for the work at hand. Despite my love for crafting stories, I wasn't a good storyteller from the start. Rather, I developed storytelling skills more quickly because the process energized me. But I still needed to seek active improvement in my storytelling to become the writer I wanted to be— and I'm still learning today.

Where strengths energize, weaknesses drain. Your weaknesses in the craft aren't necessarily the areas in which you lack knowledge or skill. Instead, they're the parts of the writing process that you don't enjoy, the ones that leave you tired rather than inspired. When confronted with parts of the writing process that wear you down, you might question whether you have what it takes to be a "real" writer. Don't let this doubt turn into a limiting belief. Remember that you're as good a writer as you work toward being. You won't enjoy every part of the writing process, but you can adopt strategies that will help you work efficiently through the more draining tasks.

I first learned this lesson for myself when, more than two years into my writing journey, I had yet to finish a first draft. "How can I be a writer if I can't get a full story down onto the page?" I wondered. After months of wrestling with resistance, I finally realized that I found the drafting process draining. Understanding this prompted me to research how other writers handle the same issue, which led me to adopt fast-drafting as part of my writing process. This weakness didn't mean that my writer card needed to be revoked. It simply signified an area in which I needed to seek intentional growth, and I did. Fast-drafting gave me the energy I needed to push through the drafting process. Five years later, I've written the first drafts of four novels, three video workshops, four email courses, one nonfiction book, and countless blog posts and newsletters.

Still, I continue to find the drafting process fatiguing, even when fast-drafting, which means drafting remains one of my writing weaknesses. No matter how well I've learned to move efficiently through this part of the writing process, my continued dislike for it leads to an increase in resistance when I sit down to write—and where resistance congregates, weakness abounds. Don't be ashamed of the weaknesses in your writing process. Every writer has them, and just because they indicate an area of increased resistance doesn't mean you're any less of a writer. What matters is that you take full responsibility for seeking intentional growth when confronted with weakness and doubt.

～

Activity: Aim for Intentional Growth

To identify areas in your writing life that need improvement, first define the strengths and weaknesses in your writing process. Ask yourself the following questions:

- Which parts of the writing process do I enjoy most?
- Which parts of the writing process do I find draining?

For example, you might enjoy or dislike crafting characters, outlining your plot, developing your story world, writing the first draft, revising your manuscript, editing your prose, or even publishing or promoting your work.

After defining your strengths and weaknesses, make a list of the skills you'd like to improve. Remember that honing your writing strengths is just as important as tackling areas of weakness in your writing ability. Now's the time to move beyond umbrella statements. Even though you love drafting, do you struggle to craft believable dialogue? Or does revising drain you because you've never understood how to critique a novel's structure? Consider these and the following elements as other possible areas where you can seek intentional growth:

- Developing character backstories or personalities
- Plotting a strong opening hook
- Crafting a believable magic system
- Writing evocative setting descriptions
- Weaving secondary plot lines into your main narrative
- Honing your narrator's voice
- Creating a book launch plan
- Running Amazon book ads

∿

An Action Plan for Intentional Growth

During this process, bear in mind the time you have to devote to self-improvement and the current depth of your creative well. If you're short on time or running low on energy, setting out to solve a major weakness in your writing life isn't a smart plan of attack. Instead, start small. Select a skill you can easily develop (e.g., learning where to place commas), or take a slow but steady approach to tackling a big-picture issue (e.g., reading one page of a book about character development every day).

If you have plenty of time and energy to devote to intentional growth, that's great. But remember that growth is difficult work. You're going to experience an increase in resistance as you develop your writing and storytelling skills. If you aim at too many targets, you likely won't hit a single one, and resistance will quickly worm its way through your resulting frustration. Instead, focus on one or two key areas of growth at a time, which will make it easier for you to "hit each target," so to speak.

With this established, it's time to create an action plan for intentional growth. Consider the following four steps as you set out to improve your writing and storytelling skills.

Step 1: Take Aim

To seek intentional growth, you must first choose the writing skill you'd like to improve. If you've completed the Aiming for Intentional Growth activity, you've already created a list of your underdeveloped skills. Review this list and determine which you'll tackle first. Keep in mind the time and creative energy you have to devote to your development, as well as which skills would have the greatest and most immediate impact on the quality of your work.

Once you've selected your top priority on this list, make

note of why you want to improve this particular skill. Will it truly help you become the writer you want to be? Or is it a reflection of a fear or limiting belief? For example, a moment of unhealthy comparison might prompt you to develop a writing style that isn't suited to your target genre. Recognizing this from the start would help you avoid a misuse of time and energy.

Examples:

- I want to improve my characterization because many of my beta readers said they had trouble connecting with my protagonist.
- I want to expand my book marketing knowledge because my newly published novel isn't selling as well as I anticipated.
- I want to improve my descriptions because I'm not quite sure how to help readers visualize a scene.

Step 2: Brainstorm Your Next Steps

It's one thing to *intend* to improve in a specific area of your writing life, but true intention demands action. So, after identifying your aim, brainstorm the steps you can take to develop that skill. For example, would it help to study the craft further, critique other writers' work, seek feedback on your own writing, or harness the problem-solving power of your subconscious? (I'll break down each of these strategies in the coming chapters.)

When preparing to take action, you might realize you can seek improvement in several ways. Choose the option that best aligns with where you are in your writing process or journey right now. If you're a new writer, you could improve your dialogue by reading books or blog articles on the topic. But if you've revised your novel several times and still doubt the quality of your dialogue, you might want to run your novel by a few beta readers instead.

Examples:

- To improve my characterization, I will seek feedback from a developmental editor.
- To expand my book marketing knowledge, I will enroll in an online course developed by a successful indie author.
- To improve my setting descriptions, I will study how other authors in my genre craft their own.

Step 3: Adjust Accordingly

Growth most often begins in a place of inexperience. Because you don't yet have the knowledge or skills you're seeking, you might discover in the course of your intentional improvement that you need to readjust your aim or action plan. Growth is about evolution, so don't be afraid to evolve.

Early in my writing journey, I set out to learn how to write better dialogue because I feared my poor writing skills resulted in contrived conversations. But as I studied the topic more, I realized that crafting believable dialogue had less to do with developing my ability to write prose than it did with getting inside my characters' heads. I readjusted my action plan to focus on learning how to develop my characters' voices and quickly fell in love with writing dialogue.

Examples:

- My developmental editor helped me realize that I haven't considered the motivations behind my protagonist's choices and behavior. I'm going to read as many resources on this topic as I can.

- The online book marketing course showed me that I'm not tailoring my listings to my intended audience. I'm going to study listings of books that are similar to mine to see how I can improve.
- Studying the setting descriptions of books in my genre revealed that my own descriptions might not be as awful as I thought. I'm going to run a few passages by my critique partner to get their opinion.

Step 4: Follow Through

In working through the first three steps of this action plan, you've learned *how* you can improve your work. Now you must implement what you've learned and apply your newfound knowledge and discoveries to your work.

Doing so isn't always easy. Developing a new skill takes time and practice, but consistent effort will yield results. Consider setting a goal or creating an action plan to guide you in manifesting what you've learned. Work with determination, and before you know it, your aim will have become an asset.

<u>Examples:</u>

- To help readers connect with my protagonist, I will create a new first chapter that shows why my protagonist wants to run away from home.
- I'm going to update my Amazon listing to feature more genre keywords and create a more enticing book description.
- I'm going to take my critique partner's advice and tailor my setting descriptions to reflect what my

point-of-view character would notice rather than a general overview of their surroundings.

You've identified your writing strengths and weaknesses, defined the skills you'd like to improve, and created an action plan to manifest that improvement in your work. Before studying the core strategies you can use to enact that plan, it's important that you first establish a strong understanding of what growth is and isn't. Here are four truths to remember about creative growth as you work toward becoming the writer you want to be.

Truth 1: Growth Is Concurrent with Creation

If you're inexperienced in your craft, you might assume that your best course of action is to flush out your weaknesses and seek to improve in each area before you start any "real" creative work. This is an illogical approach to intentional growth. You can study every resource available on any given stage of the writing or publishing process, but if you don't put that knowledge into practice—in other words, apply it to your stories and process—that knowledge won't be worth a dime. A consistent writing practice is and always will be the key to developing your skills as a writer. If you aren't writing, you won't improve your writing. It's as simple as that.

Truth 2: Growth Is Personal

In this age of online highlight reels, it's tempting to compare your journey to those of other writers, chasing what you believe is the "right" way to be a writer rather than what is best for you and your stories. Don't make the mistake of improving in someone else's game. Remember that you're building *your* best writing life. To become the writer you want to be, you must get clear about who you are as a creative and pursue what will make you great.

Truth 3: Growth Isn't Linear

Growth is an upward climb, but it's not a linear journey. Acknowledge and accept the growing pains you face, and you'll weather any turbulence you experience with patience and persistence. When turbulence does hit, take a moment to reflect on your action plan for intentional growth. It might indicate that your current aim or the strategy you're employing to achieve it is no longer the right choice for your personal development. Be mindful and adjust accordingly.

Truth 4: Growth Is an Ongoing Endeavor

Successful writers know that they will constantly work toward becoming the writers they want to be, and they embrace that reality with open arms. They know that seeking intentional growth isn't a means to an end. It's an ongoing endeavor that will define their mastery of the craft and ultimately result in the fulfillment of their personal definition of writing success.

Are you ready to embrace that same reality? To adopt the attitude of growth that will help you become the writer you want to be? Then let's get to work.

15

STUDYING THE CRAFT

Before you can think out of the box, you have to start with a box.

—Twyla Tharp,
The Creative Habit

I once asked another writer about his personal process for crafting characters.

"Oh, I don't *craft* characters," he replied, and his haughty tone caught me off guard. "I allow characters to come to me, and then I write about them."

For a moment, I blinked. This response confounded me, especially coming from a writer with several decades of experience under his belt. Was he being sarcastic? Or perhaps parodying the type of writer who thinks their work beyond reproach? As the conversation continued, I came to realize that the other writer was being honest. He believed any conscious consideration of the craft was an impediment to the muse, and he thumbed his nose at writers who believed they could study or plan their way to self-improvement.

This conversation sorely disappointed me for many reasons. On a purely technical level, I knew that a strong study of the craft could revolutionize a writer's creative ability. It had certainly done so for me. I hated knowing that at least one experienced author in the world discouraged fledgling writers from improving through active study. In truth, I wanted to shake that writer, to insist that they did indeed craft characters, whether or not they understood their own process.

You see, much of the early development of a creative work takes place in the subconscious, where inspiration brews until it bubbles over into conscious thought. This is why characters, scenes, and other story ideas might seem to spring into your awareness fully formed. But whether consciously or subconsciously developed, story ideas are always crafted—and they can always be further developed after initial creation.

This work can absolutely happen on the page. As I mentioned in chapter 9, adopting a prewriting practice isn't right for every writer's process. Characters can be developed just as well in a discovery draft as they can be in a character questionnaire. Neither approach has lesser value than the other. Nor do they contradict what it means to be an artist, because writing is both an art *and* a craft.

Storytelling requires originality and creative expression. It also requires foundational mastery. A violinist can't perform a sonata without learning their scales and arpeggios. A sculptor can't mold a spectacular piece without understanding how to work the clay. A ballerina can't move an audience without mastering pointe technique. And a writer can't produce an enthralling story without understanding the essentials of good writing and storytelling.

As I'll explain in the following chapter, you already know many of the foundational principles of the craft. You've internalized them over years of consuming stories of all shapes and sizes. But if you want to develop your writing skills, there's no better place to begin than in actively studying the craft. You don't need to apply every so-called "writing rule" to your work (and you should always question those presented to you as universal truths), but established structures and techniques exist for a reason. They're the bedrock of countless successful stories, and you can use them without sacrificing what makes your work unique.

With that in mind, let's break down the essentials of the writer's craft. The elements we'll cover in this chapter are geared mainly toward fiction writers. If you're writing memoir, biography, or another type of narrative nonfiction, you might still find the following elements beneficial to your work. If you're writing in a different medium altogether, research the elements unique to your craft and consider how you might apply them to your work.

Characterization

Character is the backbone of narrative. Your characters' goals or needs drive the plot. Their fears, flaws, and desires create engaging internal and external conflict, and their voices, personalities, and motivations compel readers to care about their stories. Without well-developed characters, readers will struggle to connect with your work and find meaning in the events taking place. When studying characterization, consider the following topics:

- Goals and motivations
- Personality and world view
- Backstory
- Voice
- The "lie" your character believes

- Character arcs (e.g., positive, negative, static)
- Character roles (e.g., protagonist, antagonist, villain, sidekick, mentor, love interest, foil)

Story Structure

One of the first story elements that readers internalize is structure: the beginning, middle, and end; a buildup to the climax; and the occasional well-placed turning point—and that's just for starters. Yet many writers fail to study the finer points of structure that can turn a promising story idea into an engaging read. They believe that applying structure to their work would result in a story that reads like every other. But structure is merely a blueprint, not a scene-by-scene breakdown of what your story should look like. It's a skeleton that you get to decide how to dress. When studying story structure, consider the following topics:

- Hook
- Inciting incident
- External and internal conflict
- Pacing
- Key event
- Midpoint
- Turning points
- Climactic sequence
- Plot and character arcs
- Resolution

Setting

Every story needs a backdrop, and every scene a time and place in which to ground its characters. But the power of setting stretches far beyond filling in the green screen of your story's scenes. A well-developed setting engages readers, creating an immersive visual that draws them further into the world you're developing. Setting can even enhance characterization, mood, tension, suspense, and other essential story elements. For writers of speculative fiction, world-building is an especially important facet of setting. It's the process of developing every element of a fictional world, from its cultures and religions to its geography, languages, and much more. When studying setting, consider the following topics:

- Mood and atmosphere
- Sensory details
- Deep point of view
- "Show, don't tell"
- Framing scenes like a filmmaker

Theme

Many writers mistake theme for a heavy-handed message that can patronize readers, and so they avoid consciously addressing themes in their work. However, a theme is simply a topic discussed throughout a story. Common themes include love, grief, power, and faith.

A thematic statement is the "message" that an author conveys about a theme, and well-developed thematic statements are rarely heavy-handed. Instead, they're implied through subtext as a story's plot and character arcs unfold. For example, a story might reveal that love conquers all, knowledge is power, or faith can heal the deepest of hurts. When studying theme, consider the following topics:

- Theme versus thematic statement
- Plot and character arcs
- The "lie" your character believes

Framework

A framework defines the parameters in which a story is told, often based on style, chronology, and point of view. Most modern stories are told through a subjective framework, meaning the author uses a limited point of view (i.e., one character's thoughts and experiences at a time) to immerse readers. Other frameworks include objective storytelling, legends, nostalgic retellings (also called frame stories), and epistolary tales. The framework in any given story has a major impact on its atmosphere and the techniques used to bring that story to life. When studying framework, consider the various frameworks listed earlier, as well as the following topics:

- Omniscient versus limited point of view
- Verb tense
- Atmosphere
- Narrators

Style and Prose

A writer's style is the culmination of their tone, word choice, sentence structure, figurative language, sensory details, and other common elements of prose. Each writer's style is unique and can vary from project to project. However, style should never usurp a writer's mastery of the general mechanics of prose. Understanding how to apply these mechanics can hone a writer's style from a place of inexperience to one of excellence. When studying style and prose, consider the following topics in addition to those mentioned above:

- Voice
- Dialogue tags
- Action tags

- Vocabulary
- Micropacing
- Head-hopping
- "Show, don't tell"

Where Should You Begin When Studying the Craft?

If you've never studied the craft of writing before, you might find these topics and their respective elements overwhelming. Take a deep breath. You don't need to master each of these overnight. Nor do you need to study all of them to gain a strong understanding of the craft. What matters is that you consider the areas in which you'd like to seek intentional growth in your writing life and then research the elements of the craft that would help you improve those skills.

When studying the craft, play to your learning style. If you're a verbal learner, read books and blogs that cover the skill you want to improve. If you're an auditory learner, enroll in an online video course, watch instructional videos on YouTube, or listen to a writing podcast. And if you learn by doing, download a writing workbook or questionnaire that allows you to practice those skills immediately. I offer many of these resources—including articles, downloadable writing workbooks, and podcast episodes that accompany every blog post I share—at Well-Storied.com.

Many writing resources cover topics beyond those listed in this chapter. For example, you can study the techniques that writers use when developing their creative processes, as well as the tropes and conventions that define the genre you write in, the structures behind compelling scenes and effective flashbacks, story elements such as motifs and pacing, and more. If there's a skill you'd like to improve, there's a resource to help you improve it. All you have to do is take an active role in studying the craft.

16

CONSUMING CRITICALLY

If you don't have time to read, you don't have the time (or the tools) to write. Simple as that.

—Stephen King,
On Writing

There is immense value in studying the writing craft. But in truth, you learned the foundations of strong writing and storytelling long before you sought your first resource on the subject. In fact, you've been learning all your life, internalizing storytelling principles from books, films, television shows, and other mediums.

With every story you consumed, you learned more about how great stories are told. You learned that they have a strong beginning, middle, and end. You learned that they hinge upon conflict, that the protagonist must want or need something, and that obstacles and antagonists will interfere along the way. You learned that tension builds into a climactic conflict shortly before the end of a story and that characters often grow and evolve as a result of their journeys. The stories you've read have even taught you how to describe a setting, vary sentence structure, use metaphors and analogies, and get inside a character's head.

All of this and more you've learned from the stories you've consumed during your life, likely without thinking twice about what you were learning. While you were kicking back with a novel or a new episode of your favorite show, your subconscious was mining insights from every line and scene you fed it. And if you can learn this much from passive consumption, imagine how you could develop your writing and storytelling skills by consuming with a critical eye.

How to Consume Critically

When most readers pick up a book, they don't consider the mechanics behind the story. They don't analyze the structure of its plot or the development of its characters. Nor do they dwell on the effectiveness of the author's writing style. That's not to say they don't have opinions about the story. Any reader could tell you whether they enjoyed a book or found the characters boring or the opening chapters too slow. But most readers don't assume the role of a book reviewer or critic and dig deep into the *why* behind the *what*. They simply move on to the next novel they're eager to consume.

Reading critically takes this to the next level. You become that book reviewer or critic and analyze what did or didn't make a story tick. This process doesn't have to be as intimidating as it might sound. In fact, there's no right or wrong way to consume critically. Analyzing a single passage can prove just as valuable in developing your writing and storytelling skills as breaking down the quality of an entire book.

Some writers take the latter approach, critiquing the quality of a book based on common story elements such as plot structure, character development, and theme. Doing so is a fantastic way to analyze how established authors treat the elements of the craft in their work and to learn how to apply their techniques to your own stories. Writers who critique on this scale often share their reviews online through their websites, newsletters, or review sites such as Goodreads. You can do this too, if you'd like.

But you don't need to write a review to critique a book. You can just as easily spend a few moments analyzing the story's elements or swapping thoughts with a fellow reader or writer. Joining a book club is another great way to consume critically. Some novels even include questions to guide book club conversation in their back matter. Don't hesitate to use these questions as the basis for your critique.

Some writers prefer to draw a line between reading for enjoyment and reading for intentional growth. Instead of critiquing a book, they select one to study when they're eager to improve a specific skill. For example, a writer might review passages from several popular books in their genre to better understand how to craft engaging action scenes. This targeted approach to consuming critically can result in more direct development of your writing and storytelling skills.

It's perfectly okay to take either or both of these approaches to consuming critically. You get to decide which is right for you based on your schedule, your preference, and the skills you're seeking to improve. To set yourself up for a successful critical reading experience, here are five tips to bear in mind.

Tip 1: Set Aside Time for Critical Reading

You don't need to be the world's most prolific reader to benefit from both the passive and active growth that reading can provide. But as a writer, books are the end product of your craft.

If you aren't reading them, how can you expect to excel in writing your own? Use the tips in chapter 7 on making time to write, and apply them when making time to read. Carving out time for reading, even if only for ten minutes a day or an hour per week, is essential to your success as a writer.

Tip 2: Acquaint Yourself with the Elements of the Craft

To analyze a story, you must first understand what you're critiquing. If you've never studied the craft of writing before, now is the time to do so. As you learn the mechanics of great writing and storytelling, you might also find it helpful to study popular book reviews on Amazon or Goodreads to gain a stronger understanding of how to analyze these mechanics.

Tip 3: Approach Critical Reading with an Eye for Personal Gain

When reading critically, remember that your intention is to improve the quality of *your* writing and storytelling. The techniques and stylistic choices that benefit one best-selling book might not prove effective in your own or align with your personal tastes, so be mindful as you apply what you learn to your work. That's not to say you should only critique books within your genre or writing style. In fact, you can learn something from any story you consume. But as you consider how to implement those lessons in your work, ensure you're doing so because the change is best for you and your stories.

Tip 4: Critique Unpublished Work

Serving as a critique partner or beta reader for a fellow writer is a fantastic way to gain experience with analyzing stories. Works in progress are often easier to critique because their rough edges are more apparent, which can help you develop your writing analysis skills and better understand which elements of your own story need work. See chapter 17 for more information on working with a critique partner or beta reader.

Tip 5: Critique Stories in Other Mediums

Unless you're writing for a visual or auditory medium, the written word should remain your primary focus when consuming critically. However, there's plenty to learn from stories in any format. The next time you watch a favorite movie or download a new podcast serial, use the same principles we discussed earlier to analyze how the creators brought their stories to life.

Get to the Root of Critical Consumption

Reading and consuming critically might seem like a monumental task, but it doesn't have to be. You might want to dive deep into critical analysis if you're struggling with a particular issue, but generally, consuming critically is a matter of consuming mindfully. In this age of instant gratification and easy access to entertainment, it's easy to consume without engaging. Have you ever cued up a show only to scroll your phone while watching? I know I have. But intentional growth isn't found in mindless consumption. To develop your writing and storytelling skills, you need to be mindful.

Be an active reader, attentive viewer, and avid listener. There's immense value in studying effective stories, as well as those that fail to live up to your expectations. Engage with both, seeking insights in the quality of the book's storytelling and the author's prose. As you do, you'll hone your inner critic, learning how to better critique your own work as you level up your writing ability.

~

Activity: Critique the Stories You Consume

When working to improve a specific writing skill, gather popular books within your genre. Study any passages that relate to this skill, asking "what" and "why" questions such as the following:

- What techniques does the author use to accomplish this skill?
- Why is each technique effective? What does it achieve?

For example, you might discover that an author uses shorter sentences for action scenes (the "what"). This sentence length mimics the staccato of the fast-paced fight, leaving no room for complex thoughts or emotions that would slow down the pace of the action (the "why"). When critiquing a book, here are several questions you can consider:

- Did the story hold your attention? What did you love about the book?
- Did the premise of the story make sense? Did the plot follow a clear progression?
- Was the story well paced? Did you grow bored, confused, or overwhelmed at any point?
- Did the characters feel real to you? Did they have strong personalities and motivations that made their choices and behaviors believable?
- Did the dialogue in the story reflect the characters' voices?
- Did the setting descriptions immerse you in the story world?

- Was the story world unique and well developed?
- Was the ending believable and satisfying? Were any threads of tension left unresolved?
- Did any parts of the book feel contrived?
- What feeling did you have upon finishing the book?

17

SEEKING CONSTRUCTIVE FEEDBACK

Feedback is the breakfast of champions.

—Ken Blanchard,
best-selling author of *The One Minute Manager*

You can't become the writer you want to be without receiving constructive criticism.

I know this is a truth you might not want to hear. To willingly seek constructive criticism is a vulnerable act. When you've completed your best work, it can be difficult to receive feedback that highlights areas in which that work needs improvement. Resistance loves nothing more than to prey upon you during this vulnerable time, encouraging you to take criticism personally, as proof that you're in some way not enough. But this couldn't be further from the truth.

Constructive criticism is exactly that: constructive. It's not arrogant, malicious, devastating, or cruel. It exists to build up, to strengthen, to help you become the writer you want to be.

This is what makes constructive criticism so essential to your growth. No matter how well you've honed your self-editing skills, you're simply too close to your work to catch many of its weaknesses. Feedback from a trusted source can make all the difference in the quality of your skills and stories if you seek and accept it with an attitude of humility.

Depending on where you are in your writing process and the type of feedback you need as part of your action plan for intentional growth, you can seek constructive criticism from the following people.

Critique Partners

Critique partners are writers who typically work within the same genre and exchange work for feedback on a frequent, ongoing basis. Every critique partnership is unique, with many critique partners also offering general encouragement and commiseration through the ups and downs of their writing lives. The one thing that all healthy critique partnerships share, however, is equal exchange. Each partner gives just as much as they receive.

Because a critique partnership is an ongoing and personal relationship, most critique partners begin as good writing friends or acquaintances. To find your own critique partner(s), consider joining a local writing group, networking with other writers at a conference or retreat, or building relationships with writers in the online writing community.

Alpha and Beta Readers

Alpha readers provide writers with feedback on individual chapters or scenes as they're written, whereas beta readers provide writers with feedback on completed drafts. Of the two, writers more commonly employ beta readers, especially after completing their first draft or after an initial revision.

Beta readers can be fellow writers, though this isn't a necessity. However, most writers seek to partner with beta (or alpha) readers who are well-read within their genre so they can receive the most insightful feedback on their work. Some writers send beta readers a list of critique questions to help guide their feedback. You can read more information about this process in the Well-Storied blog post "The New Writer's Guide to Working with Beta Readers."

Writers typically don't pay alpha or beta readers, though some writers beta-read in exchange for a fellow writer's feedback. However, it's common for writers to thank alpha and beta readers for their time and effort in their books' acknowledgments. Some writers also show their gratitude by sending each alpha or beta reader a copy of the finished book.

Because this partnership is less personal, it isn't necessary to cultivate a relationship with an alpha or beta reader before seeking their feedback on your work. Most writers find alpha and beta readers through the online reading and writing communities in which they're involved. For example, many writers have found alpha or beta readers for their work in Your Write Dream, the Well-Storied Facebook group.

Sensitivity Readers

When writers write outside their experience, especially in respect to culture, race, sexuality, gender identity, and religion (among other aspects), they often hire sensitivity readers to provide specialized feedback. Sensitivity readers are members of marginalized groups and critique the portrayal of characters belonging to their marginalization. For example, a black sensitivity reader would provide feedback on black characters written by non-black authors, or a Muslim sensitivity reader would provide feedback on Muslim characters written by non-Muslim authors. Specifically, sensitivity readers critique harmful language, stereotypes, inaccuracies, and other representation issues.

Sensitivity readers are often writers or book bloggers who offer their services through their websites. You can find a directory of sensitivity readers at writingdiversely.com/directory. If you're active in online reading or writing communities, letting others know that you're searching for a sensitivity reader can result in additional leads.

Editors

If you plan to publish professionally, you'll likely work with several editors to produce your best manuscript. The first one will often be a developmental editor (also known as a structural or content editor). A developmental editor provides in-depth feedback on the structure and content of a work. For fiction writers, this constructive criticism includes comments on a story's plot, characters, setting, pacing, and themes.

After developmental edits are complete, writers often receive feedback from a line editor who addresses the story's prose. A line editor doesn't focus on grammatical inaccuracies (though they can fix or point out such errors). Rather, a line editor provides line-by-line feedback on the style and language of a work to ensure it tells the best possible story.

Finally, copy editors provide feedback on the consistency and accuracy of a text. This isn't the same as proofreading, which ensures that a printed proof matches the finalized manuscript, contains no inaccuracies, and is formatted correctly before it's mass-produced.

If you plan to publish traditionally, your publisher will assign in-house editors to your work. But if you plan to publish independently or would like a professional edit before you query an agent or small press, you can find a list of freelance editors and editing companies at the Well-Storied blog post "An Epic Guide to Self-Publishing Resources." You can also look for editors through Reedsy, an online marketplace that connects writers with freelance industry professionals.

Book Coaches

Also called project managers or literary consultants, a book coach bridges the gap between an alpha reader and an editor, providing professional guidance through just about any struggle in your writing life, from building a writing practice and finishing a project to landing an agent or self-publishing your first book.

Though book coaches aren't utilized as often as other sources of feedback we've discussed, they're becoming more popular. Writers are recognizing how book coaches can provide the one-on-one guidance and accountability they need to achieve their personal definition of writing success. Each book coach's services are unique, so be sure to choose the coach that's right for you and your work.

I've listed several book coaches under the "Project Managers" header in the Well-Storied blog post "An Epic Guide to Self-Publishing Resources." You can also look for a book coach through Reedsy, the online marketplace mentioned above.

How to Handle Constructive Criticism with Grace

Receiving constructive criticism can be a turbulent experience. It's often difficult to hear feedback that addresses your story's weaknesses or unwittingly preys upon your creative insecurities. However, these eight tips can help make receiving and processing constructive criticism as painless as possible.

Tip 1: Adopt a Mindset of Growth

Growth happens from a place of humility. If you're willing to admit that your work isn't beyond reproach, you're already halfway to accepting feedback with grace.

Tip 2: Remember That Constructive Criticism Builds and Strengthens

Critical feedback always comes from someone who wants to help you produce your best work. Bearing this in mind when reviewing the latest notes from your editor or beta readers can make a world of difference in how you handle the inner turmoil that criticism can provoke.

Tip 3: Set Boundaries Around How You Process Criticism

Though it can be tempting to tear into criticism the moment it hits your inbox, ensure you're in the best headspace before doing so. If you're tired, stressed, or otherwise not at your best when you dive in, you're more likely to cave to any ugly lies that resistance whispers in your ear. Instead, wait until you feel calm and level-headed, then grab a glass of wine or a bar of chocolate and read through any feedback you've received in one sitting. In situations when you know you'll receive criticism in person, take care to shore up your creative mindset beforehand. Rely on affirmations that reaffirm your creative ability, and rest in the knowledge that constructive criticism is meant to help you grow as a writer.

Tip 4: Know That You Don't Have to Agree

Constructive criticism represents one person's opinion on how you can improve your work. You don't have to incorporate all such suggestions into your work. However, if you find yourself disagreeing with every piece of feedback you receive, you might need to take a hard look at your mindset. Are you reacting from a place of pride rather than considering each comment with humility? When receiving constructive criticism from beta readers, look for patterns in the feedback they provide. If several beta readers offer the same suggestion, you'll know it's one worth implementing.

Tip 5: Wait Before Making Changes to Your Work

After receiving constructive criticism, let the feedback—and your emotions—rest. Even if you agree with a critique, wait a few days to ensure you're making the best possible decision for your work.

Tip 6: Follow Up If You Have Questions

Don't let good constructive criticism go to waste over a lack of clarity. Anyone who gives you a critique of your work is there to help you succeed. Asking questions of them is a great way to ensure you understand their feedback and let them know that you value their comments and insights.

Tip 7: Make a Game Plan

The scope of the constructive criticism you receive can often be overwhelming. After several days, reassess all of the feedback, decide which suggestions you agree with, and make a plan to implement those changes in your next draft. Don't let overwhelm turn into doubt and uncertainty. Instead, focus on one element of your plan at a time, and use your affirmations or other strategies to maintain a healthy and positive mindset throughout the process.

Tip 8: Express Your Gratitude

A healthy relationship with constructive criticism begins and ends with humility. Adopt an attitude of growth going in, and share your gratitude throughout the critiquing process. Let those who have helped you know just how much you appreciate their aid. They are, after all, helping you become the writer you want to be.

18

ACCESSING YOUR FULL IMAGINATION

You get ideas from daydreaming. You get ideas from being bored. You get ideas all the time. The only difference between writers and other people is we notice when we're doing it.

—Neil Gaiman,
award-winning author of numerous novels,
short stories, comics, and films

You now know the power of intentional growth and how studying the craft, consuming critically, and seeking constructive criticism can help you become the writer you want to be. But how can you maximize your creative potential as you work toward building your best writing life? It all begins with slowing down.

Creativity blossoms in what's called a meditative state. You don't have to physically meditate to enter this state, though that's certainly a valid approach. A meditative state is simply a situation in which there are few or no demands on your mental energy and attention span. Just as you can experience growth without intention, you can benefit from a meditative state without seeking it out. Maybe you can even recall some of the times you've experienced this. Consider the many fantastic story ideas you've had while showering, driving a familiar route, or drifting off to sleep. In those moments, you were relaxed, calm, or even bored. And so, to entertain itself, your mind began to create. This is what occurs in a meditative state. You free up space for your imagination to run free. And suddenly, without any active work, you tap into your full creative potential.

Exciting, right? And here's some even more exciting news: entering into a meditative state regularly can help you maximize your creative potential. Doing so requires slowing down, which isn't always easy in the chaos of our world. Nevertheless, if you're eager to tap into the depths of your imagination, here are four techniques you can use to slow down and start creating.

Technique 1: Retrain Your Brain Through Boredom

The digital age has made it almost impossible for anyone to sit with their thoughts. When you're bored, you likely feel the itch to unlock your phone and scroll a few apps or text a friend, pick up a book or a magazine, or listen to music. Personally, I love turning on a podcast. I tune in when I walk my dog, when I get ready in the morning, when I cook dinner, and when I run errands and do chores. They're easy and engaging, and they make my day more interesting. They also detract from my ability to enter a meditative state.

Learning to resist the itch and embrace boredom is essential if you want to consciously enter a meditative state. If you relax and breathe into your boredom, allowing yourself to dwell on your creative work, your brain will seek out the creative ideas swirling in your subconscious. It will dredge up the inspiration it keeps safely tucked away from the chaos of your everyday life.

But what if you're someone who finds it difficult to sit with your thoughts? You can't expect to jump right into a deep meditative state where you'll solve all your creative problems. First, you'll need to retrain your brain to view boredom as opportunity rather than agitation.

~

Activity: Meditate to Empty Your Mind

Start with a quick meditation session. This doesn't have to be a spiritual experience. Simply sit in a quiet corner with few to no distractions, set a five-minute timer, and be still as you empty your mind. Acknowledge any thoughts that come your way, then set them aside. Focus on your breathing, the sensation at your fingertips, the relaxation in your muscles— any minute detail that requires little conscious awareness. When the timer goes off, assess your thoughts and emotions. Do you feel more creative? Did any new story ideas come your way?

~

It's okay if you don't dream up the perfect idea for the next great literary novel when you meditate. In fact, I'd be surprised if you did. The purpose of this exercise is simply to rewire your brain so it can better embrace boredom. Practice this five-minute meditation for several days in a row, then increase the length of time once you grow comfortable sitting with your thoughts. You don't have to maintain this practice for the long term. You're simply teaching yourself to slow down.

Technique 2: Get Bored, Baby!

Growing comfortable with boredom is key to creativity. Once you've practiced the meditation exercise, it's time to put that comfort to work. The next time you want to turn on a few jams, scroll social media, or play your latest audiobook, do something quieter or more meditative instead. Walk the dog in silence. Prepare breakfast without turning on your favorite song. Take a moment to sit with yourself and simply be. Invite boredom into your daily life as though it were your best friend.

As I mentioned earlier, meditative states often occur when engaging in mindless physical tasks such as driving, cooking, and showering. These tasks take the edge off boredom, giving your body something productive to do while your mind wanders. I wouldn't recommend purposefully entering a meditative state while driving, but don't hesitate to give yourself a menial task to do when spacing out, like cleaning house, taking a walk, weeding the garden, or petting your cat.

Technique 3: Use Your Meditative State to Solve Problems

Entering a meditative state is a fantastic way to brainstorm new story ideas. This can happen when you space out without a specific purpose in mind, but you can also use meditative states to solve specific issues in your work.

∾

Activity: Brainstorm Solutions While Meditating

Begin your day with a ten-minute brainstorming session. Try to solve your problem in as tangible a way as possible. Write out what you're struggling with, share it with a friend, or ponder it over your morning cup of coffee. It's okay if you don't solve your issue during this time. Set it aside, and go about your typical routine. As you enter meditative states throughout your day, you might be surprised to find how a simple solution to the problem presents itself when you least expect it.

Remember that your subconscious is a powerhouse actively working to solve the problems you present it. It's also what you access when you enter a meditative state. By removing distractions and growing comfortable with boredom, you open yourself up to receiving whatever gems your subconscious has stored in wait.

Taking ten minutes to dwell on a specific story issue will let your subconscious know that this problem is a priority it should solve. Then, as you weave in and out of meditative states throughout your day (which you've welcomed by not filling up your every waking moment with distractions), your subconscious might just throw a solution your way.

Some problems will take longer to solve. If you're dealing with a tricky plot hole or a messy world-building issue, give your brain time to work through the details. Trust in your subconscious and its ability to create, solve, and connect, and you will find the answers you're looking for.

Technique 4: Be Prepared to Take Notes

You can trust your subconscious, but you can't trust your memory. Awesome ideas are going to come your way when you enter a meditative state, and if you don't have some way to capture those ideas, you're doing yourself a disservice.

Instead of relying on your memory, carry a notebook with you everywhere so you can keep notes of new ideas when they arrive. You can also keep your smartphone handy if you don't find it to be a distraction. Between note-taking apps and the ability to record voice memos, your phone offers two fantastic ways to capture your ideas in the moment—though bringing your phone into the shower might not be ideal, of course. (That's where waterproof notepads such as AquaNotes come in handy!)

Harness the Power of Observation

Slowing down to enter a meditative state is an active rejection of awareness. In allowing yourself to be bored, you give your subconscious the limelight, encouraging it to push its greatest ideas and solutions to the forefront of your mind. But sometimes, becoming *more* aware can actually help you access a meditative state.

Consider people watching. This act of idly observing others demands a certain level of boredom and a lack of distraction. By concentrating your awareness on the people around you without actively engaging in other activities or solving a problem, you give your imagination free rein, encouraging your creativity to come out to play.

You can experience similar ways of slowing down at any time. As you drink your morning cup of coffee, consider how you might describe it using the five senses. Or, ask yourself what words you'd use to capture the color and shape of the clouds in the sky. The next time you experience heightened emotions, take a moment to observe your physical tics. What do you do when you're frustrated, angry, overjoyed, or grieving? How does your body feel and react?

If you've ever wondered how certain authors dreamed up the most vivid and realistic lines in literature—thoughts, descriptions, and interactions that are striking in their honesty

—the answer lies in observation. In slowing down, taking note, and becoming an active member of the world in which you live.

As a writer, you breathe life onto the page. But you can't achieve this mission if you don't also breathe into the world around you and into the beautiful mess of your mind. So tell me, friend: What will you create?

PART IV

THE ROAD TO WRITING SUCCESS

Success:
    : a favorable or desired outcome
    : one that succeeds

—Merriam-Webster

Make your life a masterpiece; imagine no limitations on what you can be, have or do.

—Brian Tracy

19

WHO ARE YOU AS A WRITER?

Eventually, you have to decide who you are. You have to choose your role and own that identity. We don't fake it till we make it. We believe it till we become it.

—Jeff Goins,
Real Artists Don't Starve

There are a million ways to be a writer and almost as many ways to be a successful one. This begs the question: What kind of writer do you want to be?

Every writer has a unique creative identity. In business terms, this identity is a brand. In artistic terms, it's voice and style. In both cases, your creative identity defines what makes your work unique. While some writers have strong creative identities from the start, most define and refine their identities over time. Some even reinvent themselves entirely. Regardless, understanding who you are as a writer is a vital first step in mapping your way to writing success.

When you own your creative identity, you unlock your artistic aims and interests. You open the door to understanding what you truly want from your writing life. And let's be clear: what you want might not be what other writers want or what society dictates writing success should look like. Rather, it's what will ultimately bring *you* the most joy and creative fulfillment—what defines *your* best writing life. It all begins with understanding who you are as a writer.

~

Activity: Uncover Your Creative Identity

Understanding who you are as a writer is key to mapping your route to writing success. To uncover your creative identity, answer the prompts on the following pages. Remember to be honest with yourself. Cast aside any preconceived notions of what makes a "real" writer, and consider how you would describe yourself and your work when living your best writing life.

~

Question 1: What Kinds of Stories Do You Want to Tell?

Consider this question from both macro and micro perspectives. Do you want to write literary, upmarket, or genre fiction? If you prefer the latter, which genre and subgenre do you most enjoy writing? Are you a novelist at heart, or do you prefer shorter works? What themes and story arcs do you love to explore? What kinds of characters do you most enjoy writing about?

Once you've answered these questions, try to distill those

answers into a single statement. Here's an example that encapsulates my own creative interests:

> "I write upmarket medieval fantasy fiction that features unlikely protagonists who must learn to love themselves and others as they find their places in the world, even as they're embroiled in magic and mayhem much bigger than themselves."

Question 2: Who Are You Writing For?

Again, be specific. Are you writing for a certain age group? For a person of a certain gender, sexuality, religion, or cultural background? For those living through a certain circumstance or experience? Or for a reader who is looking for a specific type of book? Once again, try to distill your answer to this question into a single statement. Here's an example from my own work:

> "I write for adults who yearn to see more emotional nuance and diversity in both character and plot in the medieval fantasy genre."

If your ideal reader is governed more by demographics, your statement might read like one of the following:

- "I write contemporary romance novels for Jewish teens."
- "I write science fiction for LGBTQIA+ readers who want to see themselves as the heroes in their favorite genre."
- "I write picture books for young children experiencing mental health and behavioral issues."

Your audience doesn't have to be defined by a specific

demographic. Even if you enjoy writing a wide variety of stories, you'll likely thread some unifying elements throughout your work. These threads will ultimately bind you to your ideal readers, the ones who will love your work no matter the stories you share. Stephen King, Nora Roberts, Neil Gaiman, and V. E. Schwab are all prime examples of authors who write for multiple age groups and within multiple genres. Yet few would deny that these writers haven't fully embraced their creative identities and, by doing so, developed avid readerships that eagerly devour everything they create.

Question 3: What Defines Your Personal Writing Style and Voice?

The terms *style* and *voice* are often used interchangeably, but the subtle differences in their definitions can offer clarity as you explore your creative identity.

A writer's style is the unique way in which they use words to capture their stories on the page. As first defined in chapter 15, style can be influenced by a writer's tone, word choice, sentence structure, figurative language, sensory details, and other elements of prose. When exploring your own writing style, consider the traits that define your writing. For example, my nonfiction writing style is instructive yet casual and friendly. It's the voice of an older sibling or an experienced friend. My fiction writing style, however, is evocative and melodic. It has a stronger ebb and flow and a darker tone. How would you describe your own writing style in a few sentences?

Voice, on the other hand, is the lens through which you write. As we first discussed in chapter 3, your writing voice is shaped by your values, beliefs, interests, experiences, and other influencing factors. I like to consider voice as the creative flavor of an author's work. And as we discussed earlier, a writer's voice is often the unifying thread that draws readers to an author's various works and continues to hold their attention as that work evolves over time.

Activity: Hone Your Creative Identity

You should have a much stronger understanding of who you are as a writer after completing the Uncover Your Creative Identity activity earlier in this chapter. To further solidify your creative identity, try combining your answers into one defining statement. For example, the following statement boils down my core creative identity as a novelist:

"I write genre-busting medieval fantasy novels for adults who love dark, character-driven narratives, evocative romance, and plenty of room for gray alongside the more traditional sword-and-sorcery hallmarks of the genre."

Honing your creative identity into a single statement can be a powerful exercise because it helps you dig deep into the heart of who you are as a writer. The better you know your creative identity, the easier it will be to sidestep unhealthy comparison, find your focus, and make the best choices for yourself and your stories. To map your route to personal writing success, make sure to refer to your statement often as you work through the remaining chapters in this book.

Finally, remember that creative identities are fluid in nature. Your stories, audience, style, and voice might evolve over time as new interests and experiences shape your work. For some, this evolution might be radical. For others, it might be a mere refinement. In either case, allowing for flexibility in your creative identity will ultimately keep you on the road to lasting writing success.

What If Your Creative Identity Is Multifaceted?

Some writers love working in various genres, writing for different audiences, or using separate styles or voice. If you're one such writer, be vigilant. There's nothing wrong with having a multifaceted creative identity. But if you discover that no unifying factor ties your work together, consider treating these projects as part of separate creative identities—or, in business terms, as individual author brands. Doing so is essential if you want to make the most of your book marketing efforts and avoid confusing potential readers.

For example, I prefer to treat my nonfiction and fiction work as individual endeavors. Not all readers who will pick up this book will enjoy my fantasy novels, because fantasy (or my unique version of it) isn't their cup of tea. It's also unlikely that those who will one day read my fantasy novels will be writers in search of guidance as they build their best writing lives. Will my audiences overlap? Sure! But if I treat them as one and the same, tailoring my work to appeal to just one specific reader, I won't make it very far in my writing life.

If you're working on two or more vastly different projects, your road map to writing success will likely see you pursuing different end goals for each project. This, and how you'll balance these various projects over time, is something to bear in mind as you map your way to writing success.

20

WHAT DOES WRITING SUCCESS MEAN TO YOU?

I learned this, at least, by my experiment: that if one advances confidently in the direction of his dreams, and endeavors to live the life which he has imagined, he will meet with a success unexpected in common hours.

—Henry David Thoreau,
Walden

D o you know what you want from your writing life?
For some, this can be a difficult question to answer. The traditional writing dream is to publish, write full-time, grow an avid readership, and perhaps hit a best-seller list or two along the way. Go on a book tour and have your work adapted for the big screen? Even better. But there's more than one way to lead a successful writing life. In fact, only one person can decide what your ideal writing life should look like: you.

The definition of writing success is highly personal. To

build your best writing life, you don't have to pursue a traditional book deal, publish for profit, or aim for household recognition. You only have to be honest. What does writing success mean to you?

~

Activity: Identify Your Personal Definition of Writing Success

To understand what writing success truly means to you, open a notebook and answer the four questions on the following pages. Be specific and honest with yourself. The more detail you provide, the clearer your path to writing success will be.

~

Question 1: Is Publishing a Part of Your Definition of Success?

Books are meant to be read. It's for this reason that most writers aim to publish their work. But if you'd prefer to keep your stories private (and if you can say with confidence that this isn't a result of a limiting belief), then keep your stories private. It's okay to write for only yourself. It's also okay to change your mind somewhere down the road.

However, if publishing is a part of your personal definition of writing success, it's important to ask why, or rather in what capacity. Publishing doesn't have to mean publishing for profit. You might want to self-publish a book solely to own a few copies for friends and family, or to publish your stories online for free simply to share them with readers.

If you do want to publish for profit, here's another essential question to ask.

Question 2: Is a Writing Career Part of Your Definition of Success?

Remember that you don't have to publish or pursue a living with your work to validate your worth as a writer. The only thing the publishing industry can validate is whether your work is marketable at one moment in time.

But if you would like to make a living with your writing, it's important that you research and answer the following questions for yourself:

- Which publishing path do I want to pursue?
- Which business model is right for my goals and niche?
- How do I plan to establish my platform and grow my readership?

These topics are big enough to tackle in books of their own. But to help you establish your initial definition of writing success, I'll give an overview of each in three upcoming chapters in the book.

Question 3: What Is Your Wildest Writing Dream?

Regardless of how you answered the first two questions, it's now time to let your imagination run wild. What is your ideal vision for your writing life? If you could achieve everything you ever wanted for your work, what would that look like? Write down everything that comes to mind.

Personally, I want to spend my life writing stories in the fantasy world I've developed. I want those stories to find a home with adoring fans who love my characters and world so much that my books are adapted as award-winning television shows in the vein of *Outlander* and *Game of Thrones*. I want to win a Hugo and a Nebula with my work. I want to be remembered.

Whatever your wildest writing dream might be, take a moment to acknowledge it. There's nothing wrong with imagining your authorial name in lights, sitting atop best-seller lists, winning literary awards, or making headlines as film or television adaptations premiere. But there's also nothing wrong with dreaming about traveling the world and creating short story chapbooks that document each country you visit, uploading fan fiction that takes the internet by storm, or penning children's stories that you spin into a successful toy company.

Achieving your wildest writing dream will be challenging and possibly outside of your control. Declare it anyway. The only sure way to fail is to not even aim your writing life in the right direction.

Question 4: What Is Your Honest Writing Ambition?

Because most writers' wildest dreams are unlikely realities, it's difficult to create a road map that leads to that version of success. To guide your writing life in a clearer direction, define a version of success that is, by most accounts, within your power to achieve. This is your honest writing ambition.

Personally, I want to write and publish my fantasy novels, slowly but surely building an income that would—if I so desired—allow to me to focus on publishing fiction full-time. That's it. That's my honest writing ambition.

Achieving this goal will still be challenging. I'll need to write and publish books with consistency and create a strong marketing plan to ensure they get into readers' hands. But with patience and persistence, I know I'll be capable of building a lucrative backlist and an avid readership. It's within my realm of control if I put in the work.

Take time now to consider your own honest writing ambition. It's okay if some aspects are out of your control. There's no guarantee you'll land an agent or a traditional book deal. But if you persist, taking care to refine and resubmit your work as you receive feedback and study the industry, there's a good chance you'll achieve these goals.

What Should You Do Next?

Between your dreams, ambitions, and publishing plan, you now have a strong idea of what you want from your writing life. If you've been honest with yourself, this definition should align with your creative identity. It's unique to you, and it will be your guide as you sketch out the details of your road map to writing success in the following chapters.

First things first: Are you ready to find your focus as you pursue your writing dreams?

21

CRAFTING A WRITER'S MISSION STATEMENT

Make your life a mission, not an intermission.

—Arnold H. Glasow,
American businessman and humor
writer for *Reader's Digest*

I n the previous chapter, you defined what writing success means to you. This is your ultimate aim for your writing life, and defining this aim is a powerful key to achieving the laser-like focus that will help you build your best writing life.

Having a clear aim in mind will help you plan your road map to writing success, but achieving that definition of success won't be easy. Somewhere down the road, you're likely to find yourself six inches deep in mud and ready to quit. When this happens, you'll need a powerful reminder of what you're working to achieve in your writing life and why you're holding onto that goal so dearly. This is where your writer's mission statement comes into play.

What Is a Writer's Mission Statement?

Companies and organizations often create short passages called mission statements to keep their customers and members informed of the aims and values under which they operate. As a writer, you can create a similar statement to distill your creative identity and your definition of writing success. This statement can then act as a reminder of your aims for your writing life, helping you stay focused and motivated in your writing journey. Pretty awesome, right?

A writer's mission statement is comprised of five key elements, with each word packing a powerful punch. As you create your own statement, try to limit yourself to one or two sentences per element, but don't be afraid to get creative. The more specific and unique your answers are to your work, the more influential your mission statement for your writing will be as a long-term motivational tool for building your best writing life.

∾

Activity: Craft Your Mission Statement

Use the prompts on the following pages to craft the five key elements that will make up your mission statement for your writing.

∾

Element 1: Your Identity

Who are you as a writer? Think back to the creative identity you established in chapter 19, then give yourself a unique title.

Here's the unique title I created for myself based on my creative identity:

> "I am a crafter of worlds and an explorer of cultures. I meld magic and meaning on the pages of my fantasy novels."

Element 2: Your Audience

Who do you write for? Pinpoint a few major interests or demographics of your ideal readers, especially those you defined as part of your creative identity. Keep in mind that you might have separate ideal readers for different projects. If so, you might want to create separate mission statements for each style of work you create. Below is the description I created for my ideal readers:

> "Fans of my work love to delve into rich story worlds and experience new perspectives on life, love, and loss, always with a sword fight or two along the way."

Element 3: Your Originality

What makes you and your work unique? Is it a special interest or skill? A life experience? A unique outlook or upbringing? Don't be shy. Celebrate what makes you *you*. My originality as a writer can be defined in this way:

> "As a medieval history geek and lover of all things romance, I bring readers into the shadows of great halls and even greater loves."

Element 4: Your Goals

Now's the time to plug in your definition of writing success from the previous chapter. What is your ultimate aim for your literary canon? The following is my big-picture goal for my fiction:

> "My passion lies in bringing my story world, Maveryn, to life via a canon of extended series, novellas, and short stories."

Element 5: Your Plan

Finally, explore how you plan to achieve your definition of writing success. You're working with only a sentence or two, so it's okay to make a broad statement. Just make sure it's clear as well. Here's a look at how I plan to achieve personal writing success:

> "I intend to publish my work independently as I introduce these stories to the world."

And voilà! Just like that, you've created a writer's mission statement to carry with you for years to come. Use this statement to inspire and motivate you as you work. You might want to write it somewhere special, set it as your computer background, or print it out to pin above your writing desk. Anywhere you'll see it often, in other words.

What does a complete writer's mission statement look like? The examples I included in this chapter are from my own mission statement for my fiction. Below is the full copy:

> "I am a crafter of worlds and an explorer of cultures. I meld magic and meaning on the pages of my fantasy novels. Fans of my work love to delve into rich story worlds and experience

new perspectives on life, love, and loss, always with a sword fight or two along the way. As a medieval history geek and lover of all things romance, I bring readers into the shadows of great halls and even greater loves. My passion lies in bringing my story world, Maveryn, to life via a canon of extended series, novellas, and short stories. I intend to publish my work independently as I introduce these stories to the world."

22

CHOOSING THE PUBLISHING PATH THAT'S RIGHT FOR YOU

My mantra, thinking of authors, is that it is good to create, better to create and publish, and best to create, publish, and monetize. May every author be successful in all these matters.

—Lee Foster,
An Author's Perspective on Independent Publishing

A re you ready to share your work with the world? If your personal definition of writing success includes publishing for profit, you'll want to consider a few hard truths before diving in.

Firstly, building a lucrative writing career is a marathon endeavor. There's no such thing as overnight success in publishing. Even on the rare occasion that a debut author rockets to stardom, that debut required years of hard work to write, revise, query, and produce. Are you willing to spend years chasing that same goal?

Secondly, contrary to popular belief, full-time authors don't spend all day writing. Successful writing careers demand readerships, and readerships don't blossom without cultivation. A large part of an author's work consists of connecting with readers and marketing their stories.

Finally, building a career on book sales alone is uncommon. Many published authors still work day jobs or find related creative work to supplement their publishing royalties. I'll share more on this topic in the next chapter.

If you're unsure if publishing for profit is right for you, check out the blog post "Can You Really Make a Living Writing Fiction?" at Well-Storied. But if you know beyond a doubt that your personal definition of writing success includes a writing career, then you need to choose the publishing path that's best for both you and your work. To make the wisest decision, it's important that you first understand how authors make a living.

Know Your Writerly Rights

As a writer, your income will stem from more than a single stream of royalties. In fact, a single book can provide a variety of income streams, including royalties from paperback, hardback, large-print, e-book, and audiobook editions, as well as foreign translations, media adaptations, and related merchandising such as workbooks, coloring books, and toys.

Publishing income is generally evergreen, meaning that as long as your book remains in print (in other words, so long as it's available for sale), you can make an ongoing profit. Media rights, on the other hand, are typically sold for a lump sum. If a contract expires, you might regain your media rights, giving you the option of reselling them for additional profit.

Trade authors—those who sell their books to traditional publishing houses for production—also receive income in the form of an advance, a lump sum agreed upon by both parties when a book deal is finalized. This lump sum is typically paid in several installments over the course of one to two years. The book must sell enough copies to cover its advance before the author will begin earning royalties.

In addition, some authors make income from selling their time or expertise via special appearances and speaking gigs related to their work. This, however, is more common among nonfiction authors who specialize in particular fields.

Trade authors and indie authors (i.e., those who self-publish for profit) hold the same writerly rights. However, these rights are often handled differently, as I'll explain later in this chapter. To understand which path is right for you and your work, it's important to note that both publishing paths are valid options for writers seeking to publish for profit. Contrary to some writers' beliefs, neither path is inherently superior to the other. Each has its advantages and disadvantages, and understanding these elements can help you choose the best path for you to pursue.

The Pros and Cons of Traditional Publishing

Trade authors have several advantages over those who choose to self-publish, including the following:

- Literary agents to champion their work and negotiate contracts in favor of their long-term success
- No upfront publication costs
- A ready-to-go team of dedicated industry professionals to produce their books
- Cash advances that they're guaranteed to earn regardless of whether the book underperforms
- Greater opportunity for industry validation in the

form of awards, reviews, and traditional best-seller
listings
- Potential marketing assistance from their publisher

Trade publishing comes with its disadvantages as well,
including the following:

- Lower royalty rates, as publishers and literary agents
take their cuts
- Infrequent paydays (royalties are typically paid twice
a year)
- Loss of creative control, as publishers most often
have the final say on a book's title, cover design,
jacket copy, and more
- A long publishing process, lasting anywhere from
one to three years from the day a book deal is signed
to the day it lands on shelves
- A hard barrier to entry, as authors must first sign
with both an agent and a publishing house before
their book is produced
- The possibility of postdeal rejection, as both literary
agents and publishing houses might drop an author
for a variety of reasons (often leaving authors'
careers in the lurch)
- Loss of rights, as trade authors sign rights away
when inking their book deals (and rights can be
difficult to regain depending on the terms of the
contract signed)
- The need to navigate an ever-evolving industry as
markets shift, in-house editors come and go,
publishing houses fold or merge, and more

The Pros and Cons of Indie Publishing

Trade authors might have the upper hand on indie authors in some respects, but the same holds true for those who choose to self-publish. The advantages of indie publishing include the following:

- Complete creative control over all aspects of a book's production and marketing
- Higher royalty rates, as most print-on-demand companies and digital distributors take smaller cuts than agents and publishing houses
- The ability to handpick their publishing team, including editors, cover designers, formatters, and other industry professionals
- A quicker publishing process (indie authors can dictate their publishing timelines and launch their books within seventy-two hours of uploading their finished manuscripts)
- More frequent paydays, as most indie authors earn monthly royalty payouts
- No gatekeepers, meaning that indie authors can publish what they want, when they want, without fear of rejection
- Full control of all of their rights unless they choose to work with a hybrid publisher
- Greater opportunity for niche publishing, as many publishing houses won't sign books that fall outside genre standards

That's not to say indie publishing is without its disadvantages, which include the following:

- Major upfront costs, as indie authors must pay out

of pocket to have their books professionally
produced (i.e., edited, proofread, formatted, and
designed)
- The responsibility of choosing a reputable
publishing team, as most indie authors work with
freelancers or small companies that must be vetted
to ensure their credibility
- Potential financial loss, as indie authors might not
recoup upfront costs if they fail to properly market
their work
- Self-publishing stigma, which is fading but still
persists among some readers and writers and within
the public consciousness
- No agent support, though some indie authors do
sign with agents to assist in selling foreign and
media rights
- Full marketing responsibility, which demands that
authors view themselves as entrepreneurs as well as
writers

Which Publishing Path Is Right for You?

In a few chapters, I'll share how you can create your personal
road map to writing success. But to do so, you'll need to understand your true definition of writing success. If you're planning
to build a writing career, this includes knowing the publishing
path you'll pursue.

Take time now to consider the pros and cons outlined in
this chapter. If you gravitate toward a specific publishing path,
ask yourself why. Are you only interested in traditional
publishing because of the validation you believe agents and
publishers can provide? Consider all of the poorly written
books that manage to nab deals, and you'll realize the only validation trade publishing can give lies in how marketable agents

and publishers believe your book might be at that moment in time. On the other hand, are you interested in pursuing indie publishing because you're repulsed by the idea of giving up creative control? If you're too precious about your work, your ego might stand between you and success no matter which publishing path you choose.

When considering which path is right for you, set aside any preconceived notions and weigh the pros and cons of each option. Do your research. The information shared in this chapter is an overview of the advantages and disadvantages of trade and indie publishing. For more information, you might want to peruse the articles I've shared on publishing at the Well-Storied website. I also recommend books such as *Let's Get Digital* by Dave Gaughran, *Publishing 101* by Jane Friedman, and *How to Make a Living with Your Writing* by Joanna Penn.

Making the best decision for your publishing future will take time and effort, but don't hesitate to do your due diligence. You can't build your best writing life if you're pursuing a publishing path that isn't right for you.

∼

Activity: Choose the Publishing Path That's Right for You

Though many factors are at play when deciding which publishing path to pursue, most factors fall into one of four categories: time, money, creative control, and validation. To gain clarity as you determine which publishing path is right for you, answer the following questions:

- How much do I value the freedom to publish on my own schedule?
- Am I willing to risk financial loss to retain more of my publishing profit?

- Is it important to me to retain full creative control of my work?
- Do I crave the external validation of traditional publishing success?

Weigh each question carefully, and be honest with yourself. Publishing is a highly personal journey, and no path is better than another. Take the time to ensure you choose the path that's best for you and your work.

23

BUSINESS MODELS FOR AUTHORS

*Being a starving artist is a choice, not a necessary condition of
doing creative work.*

—Jeff Goins,
Real Artists Don't Starve

I f part of your personal definition of writing success
includes making a living from your writing, here's the good
news: you can build a successful career as an author in many
ways. To do so, you must think of your work as a business. Your
books are your products, and your readers are your customers
—and books don't sell themselves. Are you willing to adopt an
entrepreneurial spirit to make a living from your writing?

This question doesn't just apply to indie authors, who must
finance the production and marketing of their own books. The
rise of independent publishing has eaten into the profits of
traditional publishers, leading publishing houses to make

major cuts in their marketing departments. Though trade authors do benefit from their agents' guidance and their publishers' expertise, many must still take charge of spreading the word about their books.

How you go about marketing your work and building your readership will depend largely on the work you create. Though every author's experience will be unique, most writers tend to build their careers around one of four business models that aligns with their writing niche and interests. If you plan to publish for profit, choosing the business model that's right for you and your work is an essential step in setting yourself up for a successful career.

The Four Elements of an Author Business Model

A business model is a plan for the successful operation of a business and is comprised of four major elements: products, income streams, customer base, and financing.

An author's products are the books they write and any related products they sell and/or services they offer. Some products can have multiple income streams. For example, a single book can lead to income from print, e-book, audiobook, large-print, and workbook editions. Other author income streams include foreign language and media rights, teaching and services, appearances and speaking gigs, and patronage. An author's customer base is, of course, their readership—especially their ideal reader—while their financing indicates how they'll pay for book production and marketing expenses, career-related travel, and other business costs.

If you've read through the previous chapters in this book, you've already defined the types of stories you're interested in writing and the readership you'd like to build. You've also decided whether you or a publishing house will finance your production expenses. The remainder of this chapter will help you define how you'll build income streams by breaking down the most common ways authors make their livings.

Business Model 1: High-Volume Publishing

With high-volume publishing, authors focus on building income via book sales by publishing frequently—often several times a year—in highly commercial markets.

For fiction, the most commercial works are novels that adhere to strict genre conventions. These books are often referred to as "genre fiction," "commercial fiction," or "pulp fiction." High-volume fiction can still fall into niches within popular genres—such as paranormal romance, international thrillers, or sword-and-sorcery fantasy—but those niches should be well established and thriving.

The most commercial nonfiction works are short prescriptive or self-help books that guide readers in resolving pain points in their personal or professional lives. Popular topics include self-development, spirituality, technology, hobbies, finance, relationships, and health.

Authors who choose high-volume publishing are often able to support themselves on book sales alone after establishing their backlists, though ongoing marketing techniques are often essential to their continued success. Examples of authors who use this business model successfully include Nora Roberts, Adam Croft, H.M. Ward, Lisa Kleypas, and Rick Riordan.

This is the first and only author business model that features income streams based entirely on book sales. As I mentioned in the previous chapter, it's rare that an author makes a living from book sales alone, especially in the early years of their careers. The three remaining business models in this chapter show how you can build a writing career even if your personal definition of writing success doesn't see you relying on high-volume publishing.

Business Model 2: Publishing and Teaching

Another way to build a writing career that's popular among nonfiction authors is to supplement book sales with teaching. Typically, an author positions themselves as an authority on a topic and publishes books related to this topic while supplementing that income with speaking, consulting, and/or selling relevant products such as digital workbooks, video courses, and online workshops.

This is the business model I currently employ for my nonfiction work. As of publication time, I make the bulk of my income from digital products, which was the focus of my original creative business plan. I'm now transforming my business model to focus on publishing while continuing to use these products as supplemental income.

Many other models exist within the teaching umbrella that you can use as a basis for your creative business. Some nonfiction authors use book sales to supplement their speaking or consulting income rather than the other way around. Some publish a series of related books, while others use one book as the basis of their teaching empire. Others operate under an entirely different model. Before creating your road map to writing success in chapter 25, research these and other business models to determine which one fits you best. This can be as simple as entering "nonfiction business model" into your search engine of choice and reading the results.

Examples of authors who use this business model successfully include Julia Cameron, Mark Dawson, Joanna Penn, Mel Robbins, and SARK.

Business Model 3: Publishing and Patronage

Many less prolific authors, especially those writing literary or upmarket fiction, turn to patronage to supplement their publishing income. Patronage can come in the form of grants and fellowships, residencies, or direct-from-reader support via sites such as Patreon. In recent years, the award money earned from winning literary prizes has also proven a patronage of sorts for some authors. Examples of authors who use this business model successfully include George Saunders, N. K. Jemisin, Seanan McGuire, and Saladin Ahmed.

Business Model 4: Supported Publishing

One of the surest ways to build a writing career is to publish while supporting your career with a standard day job until your backlist and author platform are strong enough to support themselves. This is a different business model than high-volume publishing. Though your focus remains solely on book sales, you don't have to publish at a high volume to build your career. You can, over many years, build a strong backlist and use smart marketing techniques to forge a stable writing career that will one day prove lucrative enough to replace your day job.

This slow-and-steady approach is frequently favored by fiction writers who don't want to pursue high-volume publishing and who don't write in niches that allow for teaching or traditional patronage. This business model is also the most common approach writers take to building their careers. Many authors, even best-sellers, still hold day jobs as they build their backlists and publishing income. There's no shame in this. A stable day job is a fantastic investment in your writing career. The steady income allows you to focus on writing rather than whether your book sales will cover your bills. In turn, you'll build your best writing life more quickly.

Some writers escape their corporate day jobs by building creative businesses in addition to their writing careers or by pursuing freelance writing, all while slowly building their backlists. This is a form of supported publishing as well, since that income is entirely separate from book publishing and requires its own business model.

Examples of authors who use this business model successfully include Anne Rice (former insurance claims examiner), Diana Gabaldon (former university professor), Haruki Murakami (former jazz club manager), and John Green (former publishing assistant and production editor).

Which Business Model Is Right for You?

This depends on your personal definition of writing success. For example, if you want to publish a large backlist of books within your favorite fiction or nonfiction genre, consider a high-volume business model. If you want to build a creative business as an authority in your field, then pursue a model that allows you to publish and teach. Supplementing your publishing income with patronage might be a great option if you'd prefer to write literary or upmarket books. Last but not least, you can always support your publishing dreams with a full- or part-time job if you'd rather slowly but surely build your writing career.

Note that the lines between these business models can blur. Many writers support their high-volume publishing with a day job until they've established their backlist. Some nonfiction authors and teachers use patronage to build a community with their readers and students. Other writers pursue separate brands and business models as they write in two or more different niches.

Hopefully, in reviewing the four business models outlined in this chapter, you'll find one that clearly aligns with your niche and interests. However, you can also blend elements of several business models into one that works best for you and your creative mission.

Activity: Define Your Authorial Business Model

Consider what writing success means to you, as well as which publishing path and business model (or blend of elements from several business models) is right for you and your work. With these items in mind, answer the following questions:

- What products will I produce as an author?
- Which authorial income streams will I pursue?
- Who is my intended market?
- How will I finance my business operations?

Answer these questions in as much detail as you can. The more specific you are about your business model, the clearer your road map to writing success will be.

Remember that building a writing career is a marathon endeavor. Most writing careers take years—even decades—to build, and that can be a tough pill to swallow. It might be tempting to pursue a high-volume business model simply because it's the fastest route to an income based solely on book sales, but if you aren't passionate about writing within a highly commercial genre, you're going to burn out fast. And because you aren't writing from a place of passion, any books you do publish likely won't hold the same appeal as those written by authors who love their work.

No matter what, don't let the lengthy business timeline of publishing frighten you away from pursuing your writing dreams. If making a living with your writing is an essential element in your personal definition of writing success, then it's worth pursuing. You certainly won't become the writer you want to be without getting started, so choose the author business model that's right for you, then get to work. You've got a career to build, writer.

24

GROWING AN AVID READERSHIP

Writing is about you. Publishing is about the book. Marketing is about the reader.

—Joanna Penn,
Successful Self-Publishing

The only way a book gets read is if someone makes the effort to connect that book with its ideal reader, and the best person to make that connection for your book will always be you. You know your book more intimately than any other person. You know exactly who will love your work. And if you put forth the time and effort to get your book into the hands of your ideal readers, you'll grow an avid readership who will eagerly consume each and every book you write.

If you're planning to publish for profit, growing this kind of audience is likely part of your personal definition of writing success. Doing so is also the basis of book marketing, an activity many writers shy away from rather than embracing. Marketing often receives a bad rap as a heartless, sales-driven cash grab, but this doesn't have to be the case. In fact, it shouldn't. Is the purpose of book marketing to sell more books? Absolutely. But you can't sell books to just anyone.

In marketing your book to its ideal readers, you connect those readers with a book they'll love, making marketing just as much about readers' happiness as it is your own financial success. And if you're preparing to publish (or if you're already building your writing career), marketing your work should be an ongoing part of your writing road map.

How Do You Market Your Work?

The more visible you are as a writer, the more opportunities you'll have to connect your work with readers. The process of gaining visibility is also known as building an author platform. On her website, publishing professional Jane Friedman defines an author platform as the "ability to sell books because of who you are or who you can reach."

For nonfiction writers, it's beneficial to establish an author platform before publishing, typically in the form of a successful blog or podcast, a career as a speaker or social media influencer, or authority in a specific field. Having an established platform gives that author the credibility they need to market their specialized work to readers.

However, fiction writers don't need to build strong platforms before publishing. Rather, their books *are* their platforms. With every story an author shares, they build their body of work and their credibility as an author worth reading. The more books an author publishes, the more visibility that author will gain. There are exceptions: some debut authors skyrocket into public awareness, while some longtime authors fail to build meaningful connections with readers. But in most cases, nothing will help a fiction author more than an established body of quality work that's ready and available for readers to consume.

How to Position Your Work for Consumption

Readers can't read your books if they don't know your books exist. They also won't want to read your books if your books aren't appealing at first glance.

If you plan to pursue traditional publishing, your work will likely be well positioned for consumption, especially if you land a deal with a big-name publisher. The backing of a publishing house offers credibility to your work; with some luck, the design and marketing teams at your publisher will produce a great cover and jacket copy to hook new readers. Beyond this, it's your job as a trade author to work with your agent and publishing house to ensure your book receives as much visibility as possible before and after it launches. Bear in mind that publishers often have large production schedules. Sometimes good books get lost in the shuffle, so be proactive about seeking opportunities to get your book into readers' hands.

If you choose to publish independently, you must give credibility to your own work, and publishing a book that can rival its traditional counterparts in both quality and production is key. That quality should extend to your marketing as well, beginning with a fantastic title, cover, and jacket copy. These three elements are your primary marketing tools. It doesn't matter how many readers discover your book's listing. If they aren't hooked by these three elements, they won't buy your book—and they'll never know whether it could have been a lifelong favorite.

Once a book is well positioned for consumption, it's time to market that book to extend its visibility and reach more of your ideal readers. Here are five core book marketing tips that will help both trade and indie authors build and maintain avid readerships.

Tip 1: Tailor Your Listings

You can't just slap your book up on Amazon and expect to reach your book's ideal readers. If you're publishing your work independently, remember that no detail should be overlooked. Each category and keyword is an opportunity to position your book to the right readers, as is your pricing model and author bio. Take care with each of these elements. Do your research, then use your listings to your advantage.

Tip 2: Use Your Books as Marketing Tools

Nothing sells your first book—and builds your readership— better than the second. Part of the reason for this lies in the power of a backlist, which, as I mentioned earlier, establishes your credibility and builds the author platform you need to reach more readers. But each book you publish also holds fantastic marketing potential, specifically in your book's back matter: the pages that come after the main body of your book.

Back matter is a fantastic place to tease readers with more material. Consider how many books include an "Also by the Author" page or an excerpt from another of the author's works. You can also use your book's back matter to inform readers about your email list (which we'll cover next) and encourage them to sign up by offering a free bonus, such as a related short story, novella, or teaser.

Tip 3: Harness the Power of an Email List

No one subscribes to receive more emails unless they believe they'll find immense value in what they'll receive. This means that every reader who subscribes to your email list wants to hear more from you. They're an interested reader or an avid fan. And next to publishing more books, there's no better way to market your work than to engage with the readers who love it most.

Readers are incredibly passionate. If they find a book they love, they'll shout about it from the rooftops—and if they get to know and love the author behind that book, they'll share that love with even more enthusiasm. This is what makes an email list so powerful; it's a direct line to your most ardent fans, the ones who have the power to lead new readers to your work. And you don't have to cultivate a big list for it to be effective— and, by extension, lucrative. A few passionate readers can create a *lot* of hype.

To maintain your list, take care to connect with subscribers on a frequent and consistent basis. (Once or twice a month is common.) In your emails, you can share anything from exclusive looks at your writing process to snippets from your works in progress, book sale announcements, meetup opportunities, and news about upcoming books.

Tip 4: Establish an Author Website

An author website is a writer's online information hub. It's where new and avid fans alike can learn more about you and your work, making it an invaluable marketing tool. Note that an author website isn't a blog. Most author websites exist solely to share information about the author and their work and to give readers the opportunity to buy the author's books, subscribe to their newsletter, and learn more about how they can connect with the author in person and online.

You can include a blog on your author website, if you'd like. Nonfiction authors can benefit from this practice, as blogging can be a form of content marketing. But for most fiction authors, blogging is unnecessary. The amount of time it takes to run a successful blog isn't worth the effort from a marketing perspective. Most novelists who do write blogs use them solely to share updates and announcements, often labeling their blogs as such in their site's navigation.

Tip 5: Build Your Social Presence

While creating and maintaining a social media presence isn't essential, it's an excellent way for authors to connect more personally with longtime fans. It also presents an opportunity to reach new readers, though word-of-mouth recommendations and the Amazon search engine remain the most common ways readers discover new-to-them books and authors.

If you want to use social media to increase your visibility and connect with readers, start small and build accounts where your ideal audience exists. For example, the readers who follow an author on Instagram aren't always the same ones who like that author's Facebook page. Whenever possible, try to engage on platforms you enjoy. Laboring away on a site that isn't your style can be draining in the long run, whereas interacting online in a way that you like is an energizing and sustainable practice.

Growing an Avid Readership Means Marketing Your Work

If you expect to reach thousands of readers upon publishing your first book, you'll be sorely disappointed. Building a writing career and an audience to sustain it takes time. To thrive in this marathon endeavor, remember that slow but steady wins the race. Take one task at a time. Climb your learning curves. Establish systems that simplify your marketing efforts, and keep studying the ever-changing industry.

Most importantly, try to create balance between writing books your readers will love and marketing those books to ensure they get into readers' hands. Every writer's definition of balance will look a little different. For some writers, it's alternating between writing and marketing for weeks or months at a time. For others, it's developing a few well-honed habits that allow them to engage in both endeavors on a daily or weekly basis.

Finding the marketing strategy that works best for you is much like defining your personal writing process. Some methods might align with your natural tendencies, while others will require a test-drive to see if they're the right fit. Don't be afraid to explore other strategies and ditch those that no longer serve your needs—or rather the needs of your readers. If you put consistent effort into marketing in honest and engaging ways, you'll grow a readership that will rave about your work for years to come.

∿

Activity: Grow Your Avid Readership

Consider the five book marketing tips shared in this chapter. Which would have the most immediate impact on your visibility and reach? If you're new to marketing, start by tailoring your listings and establishing your author website. If you're further into your career, consider launching (or improving) your email list and forging deeper connections with your readers on social media.

If you're new to book marketing, be mindful about

learning effective strategies. Research is your friend. Myriad books, blogs, and information products are available to help you learn common book marketing techniques. Some of my favorites include Joanna Penn's *How to Market a Book*, Tim Grahl's *Your First 1000 Copies*, and Mark Dawson's e-courses "Ads for Authors" and "List Building for Authors." For more guidance on book marketing, read the next chapter to learn how to create your road map to writing success.

25

CREATING YOUR WRITING ROAD MAP

You can measure your worth by your dedication to your path, not by your successes or failures.

—Elizabeth Gilbert,
Big Magic

Y ou've done your prep work. You've learned how to hone a healthy creative mindset, build a sustainable writing practice, and harness the power of intentional growth. You've defined your creative identity and what writing success means to you. If your definition of success includes publishing for profit, you've also considered the publishing path and author business model that best suit you and your work, as well as the principles behind growing an avid readership. Now the time has come to create your road map to personal writing success: a step-by-step plan for achieving the goals and dreams that define your best writing life.

Don't underestimate the power of a writing road map. It's

essential to know what you want from your writing life, but you'll never build that life if you don't know how. If you focus solely on your big-picture goals and dreams, you're unlikely to achieve them. But when you take a big-picture goal—such as writing a book, landing a book deal, or building a writing career—and treat it as a destination rather than a someday dream, you can make a step-by-step plan for arriving at that destination. In other words, you can make your best writing life a reality.

The beauty of a writing road map is its simplicity and flexibility. When properly developed, a road map gives you the focus and determination you need to circumvent resistance and move toward the writing life you'd like to lead—and it does this without hemming you in to one particular route or final destination. Because a writing road map centers on the here and now, you can easily revise your road map to match your evolution in your writing process, creative identity, or personal definition of writing success.

Creating your writing road map requires that you complete three simple steps. To begin, you'll define the first landmark in your journey to writing success. You'll then set the mile markers that will serve as progress points en route to your destination. Finally, you'll identify the benchmarks that will make the long journey seem not only manageable but enjoyable.

Step 1: Define Your First Landmark

No matter your personal definition, writing success is a destination set somewhere over the horizon, far beyond immediate reach. To arrive at this definition, you'll need to journey many days and nights over rocky terrain, facing obstacles that might force you to question your destination or your ability to reach it. This is where a writing road map can make all the difference.

To avoid the stress, fear, and overwhelm that can come with traveling toward such a destination, your first step is to define a much closer vantage point in your path to success. This is your first landmark, a goal you can reasonably achieve within one or two years that will mark major progress in your journey toward writing success.

Examples of First Landmarks

- Complete your current work in progress.
- Sign with an agent.
- Self-publish your novel.
- Sell your first one thousand copies of your book.
- Establish your online author platform.

Step 2: Set Your Mile Markers

Reaching the first landmark in your writing journey can still be overwhelming. Writing a cohesive and compelling novel is hard work, landing an agent can be as difficult as finding a needle in a haystack, self-publishing a high-quality book takes time and effort, and successful book marketing comes with a steep learning curve. It's no wonder the first bump in the road sends so many writers off course.

To keep your feet pointed in the right direction, the second step is to set your mile markers. These are tasks you can complete within a few weeks or months as you work toward the first landmark in your journey. Set as many mile markers as you think you need to reach that landmark.

Examples of Mile Markers

To complete your current work in progress, you might take the following steps:

1. Finish the first draft.
2. Revise the manuscript.
3. Seek constructive criticism from beta readers.
4. Revise the manuscript again.
5. Complete a final polish.

To sign with an agent, you might take the following steps:

1. Write a query letter.
2. Compile additional submission materials, such as your synopsis and sample chapters.
3. Compile a list of agents who might enjoy your work.
4. Submit your work to several agents at a time.
5. Refine your query based on agent feedback.
6. Continue submitting until you land the right agent for your work.

Step 3: Identify Your Benchmarks

Even mile markers can be difficult to reach when the road turns rocky. This is why the final step in creating your writing road map is to identify your benchmarks, or goals you can easily attain each day or week as you work toward your first mile marker. These benchmarks provide a daily sense of accomplishment and momentum, encouraging you to keep pushing forward even when the road ahead looks daunting. Even when it feels like you still have a long way to go on your path, reviewing these benchmarks can remind you that you're only a few steps away from celebrating another achievement.

A benchmark can consist of a task or a goal that hinges on input or output. For example, you might want to hire a cover designer or send three query letters (tasks), write for thirty minutes a day or complete three hours of marketing work this week (input goals), or revise one thousand words by Friday (output goal).

Just remember that goals based on output can be problematic when they favor quantity over quality. If you find that aiming for a benchmark based on output creates unhealthy pressure in your writing life, consider setting an input-based goal instead.

Examples of Benchmarks

To finish your first draft, you might take one of the following actions:

- Commit to writing for at least twenty minutes a day.
- Draft three chapters a week.
- Write one thousand words every Monday, Wednesday, and Friday.

To write a query letter and compile additional submission materials, you might take the following steps:

1. Research how to write an effective query letter.
2. Write the first draft of your query letter.
3. Revise your query letter.
4. Seek feedback on your query letter from an experienced critique partner or editor.
5. Refine your query letter based on the feedback you receive.

Using Your Road Map

A writing road map is a reference document. You're meant to refer to it often and let it guide you. Make a habit of reviewing your road map every day to note the next step in your journey and remind yourself of the big-picture goals you're working toward. The more you visualize these destinations as ones you'll reach, the more real they'll become in your mind. You aren't on a *maybe* path or a *someday* journey. You're on the road to building your best writing life. Let that reality become a driving force for you.

Remember that a writing road map is also an evolving document. The achievements that define your landmarks, mile markers, and benchmarks can and should evolve the further you progress in your writing journey. This is another reason why you should refer to your road map on a daily basis. When you achieve each benchmark that will help you reach a mile marker, you can then map out the next leg of your writing journey. And when you've passed enough mile markers to arrive at your first landmark, you can create a new writing road map to guide you to your next landmark.

~

Activity: Reflect on Your Writing Life

Each time you tailor your writing road map to guide you toward a new mile marker or landmark, you might find it helpful to also reflect upon your writing life as a whole. When you do, ask yourself the following questions:

- What does my creative mindset look like? Do I need to address any new doubts or limiting beliefs?
- Is my current writing practice still working for me? Do I need to make any adjustments to my writing schedule, process, or creative workspace?
- Have I taken time to refill my creative well lately?
- How am I seeking intentional growth? Which area

of my writing life would I like to improve in the coming weeks or months?

- Am I still energized by the work I'm creating and by my current definition of writing success?

Remember to pace yourself as you follow your road map to writing success. Though the road ahead will have its ups and downs, you're in for an incredible journey, one that promises endless joy and fulfillment if you only take a moment to seek it out, to breathe into the beauty of each step along the way.

The landmarks and destinations you reach might prove to be the most thrilling achievements in your writing life. But in truth, your best writing life is here and now. It's in each word you write in the face of resistance, in the confidence you cultivate in your skills and stories, in your commitment to consistently work toward becoming the writer you want to be. "It's like discovering that while you thought you needed the tea ceremony for the caffeine," wrote Anne Lamott in *Bird by Bird*, "what you really needed was the tea ceremony."

WRITING ROADMAP EXAMPLE 1

To land a book deal with one of the Big Five publishers, I will take the following steps:

Step 1: Define Your First Landmark

1. Finish my current work in progress.

Step 2: Set Your Mile Markers

1. Finish the first draft.
2. Revise the manuscript.
3. Seek constructive criticism from beta readers.
4. Revise the manuscript again.
5. Complete a final polish.

Step 3: Identify Your Benchmarks

1. Commit to writing for at least twenty minutes a day.

WRITING ROADMAP EXAMPLE 2

To establish a successful career as an indie author, I will take the following steps:

Step 1: Define Your First Landmark

1. Publish my first novel.

Step 2: Set Your Mile Markers

1. Hire an editor to proofread my manuscript.
2. Format the final manuscript for print and e-book distribution.
3. Commission cover design for print and e-book editions.
4. Create my listings on book distribution sites.
5. Upload my final print and e-book files, verify my settings and information, and publish the listings.

Step 3: Identify Your Benchmarks

1. Research freelance editors who offer proofreading services.
2. Query my first choice, and sign a contract for the work.
3. Send the editor my manuscript before their project start date.
4. Review and approve the formatted manuscript, and receive the final files.

WRITING ROADMAP EXAMPLE 3

To build a lucrative fiction writing business, I will take the following steps:

Step 1: Define Your First Landmark

1. Establish my online author platform.

Step 2: Set Your Mile Markers

1. Create my author website.
2. Establish a presence on social media.
3. Build my email list.

Step 3: Identify Your Benchmarks

1. Research personal website platforms, and choose the one that's best for me.
2. Set up my account, and purchase a domain name.
3. Create the pages on my website, and add copy (i.e., text) to each page.
4. Tweak the design, and upload images.
5. Add links to my published books.

CONCLUSION
WRITING SUCCESS STARTS TODAY

As Wesley says to Buttercup in *The Princess Bride*, "Life is pain, Highness! Anyone who says differently is selling something."

Your writing life doesn't have to be inherently painful, but never let anyone tell you that building your best writing life is easy. You've already taken pains to become the writer you want to be. You've honed a healthy creative mindset. You've developed a writing practice you love. You've learned to wield tools for intentional growth, and you've laid out your personal road map to writing success.

That work is nothing to scoff at, and it's my greatest hope that you're proud of the strides you've made in these endeavors. In completing this work, you've established a lasting foundation on which to build your best writing life, and that's worth celebrating.

Still, you'll need to accept one more difficult truth: all the hard work you've put into building your best writing life while reading this book doesn't guarantee creative fulfillment or long-lasting success. You're still going to struggle against the pull of resistance. You're still going to encounter difficulties in your projects and writing process. You're still going to face criticism and rejection, and some goals might forever remain out of your reach. Life is pain, and sometimes you'll experience that pain in your writing life. Don't let this deter or defeat you.

At this point, I could share a thousand encouragements to bolster you for the work ahead, like "the strongest steel is forged in the hottest fire," or "if at first you don't succeed, try, try again." But when it comes to finding the determination to work through trials and turmoil, the mantra I find most encouraging is one that might be new to you: *ad astra per aspera*, or "to the stars through difficulty."

Are You Ready to Chase Your Stars?

Building your best writing life is an ongoing endeavor. It's a process that happens every time you sit down and do the damn hard work, as you become—through every word you write— the writer you want to be.

That's why you should find reasons to enjoy the journey. To find fulfillment in the process rather than forever seeking it in your next big goal. There won't be a day when you can kick back, sigh happily, and say, "I've made it as a writer. I'm successful now." Instead, there will always be another hill to climb, another goal to reach, a new star to chase. Work toward them, but learn to love each and every day of your writing life as well, no matter the difficulties they bring, because the milestones you reach are mere moments in the grand scheme of your writing life. It's in embracing the daily creative process that you'll find your joy.

Appreciate the good days and the bad. Put the principles in this book into practice, and remember to view doubts and missteps as opportunities for growth. Look at difficult writing sessions as stretch days for your creativity and motivation, and take pride in every bit of progress, no matter how big or small. Success is within your grasp, my friend.

Your best writing life begins today.

AUTHOR'S NOTE

Writer, thank you for picking up this book. I hope these pages have inspired and empowered you as you journey toward building a writing life you love. If that's the case, would you consider reviewing *Build Your Best Writing Life* on Amazon? A simple one-line review can go a long way toward helping this book reach new readers and thrive.

Thank you for supporting my work in this way!

For even more writerly insight and encouragement, be sure to join my email list at www.well-storied.com/subscribe. I use this weekly newsletter to share insider-only advice on the craft, updates on new books and blog posts, and access to exclusive email courses and other free digital resources.

ACKNOWLEDGMENTS

I wrote this book to help fellow writers build their best writing lives, but if I know one thing for certain, it's that writing this book has helped me build my own.

For years, I wanted to write a book for writers, but I didn't believe I had the ability to do such a book justice. Perhaps that belief was founded in some measure of truth. I couldn't have written this book without first learning to cultivate confidence in my skills or developing those skills through intentional practice. So when I finally did put figurative pen to paper, writing this book prompted immense pride and creative fulfillment.

Still, I couldn't have written this book without the aid of an army of incredible people. First, there are my beta readers, the brave souls who volunteered to read and critique an early draft of this project that was, um, far from pretty. My unending gratitude goes out to Alli Agro-Paulson, Leftie Aubé, Jonathan Baldie, Molly Krasel, Danielle Urick Carriere, Romain Cochet, Michelle Cornish, Amanda DiCastri, Diana James, Kate Johnston, Jennifer Laird, Jen Lasalle, Trisha Lian, Abigail Marquez, Cate Townsend, and Erik Williamson. Your feedback was invaluable in shaping this book. Thank you.

My gratitude also goes out to Sara Letourneau, who painstakingly polished the rough edges of this book line by line and whose enthusiasm and encouragement never ceased to keep me smiling through some of the most tedious parts of the editing process. I also want to thank Sarah Kolb-Williams for her excellent work copy-editing and proofreading this book, as well as Jelena Mirkovic Jankovic (also known as Boja) for understanding my vision for this book's cover and executing it to perfection. Additionally, I'd like to give a special shout out to my Patreon patrons, including Stephanie L. and Victoria Fry, without whom this book wouldn't exist. Thank you for supporting this project so selflessly.

I'd be remiss if I didn't also thank my mom, unshakeable rock that she is, who never once wavered in her belief that I could—and can continue to—become the writer I long to be. Thank you for believing in this book. Thank you for believing in me.

Finally, to my wonderful Well-Storied community. You have given my life incredible joy and purpose. It is an honor to create for you and to be created by you in return. Thank you for shaping me into the writer I am today.

CREATIVE AFFIRMATIONS

The following is a list of the creative affirmations included throughout this book, as well as a few additional favorites that didn't find their way into any particular chapter. Consider using these affirmations to address your limiting beliefs and cultivate creative confidence.

You may also wish to develop your own affirmations to confront the unique ways in which resistance manifests in your writing life.

~

I write. Therefore, I am a writer.

I will build my best writing life because writing energizes and excites me.

I am as good a writer as I work toward being.

All progress is good progress.

I am capable of completing difficult creative work.

I am defined not by creative turbulence but by my commitment to my craft.

I am becoming the writer I want to be.

My work is original because I am the one writing it.

I write the stories I want to read, and that is good enough.

I will be someone's favorite writer.

Every story, including my own, has an audience.

I deserve to write what I love regardless of what others think.

Every word I write teaches me to be a better writer.

I will write happily and freely because done is better than perfect.

When I pursue my passion for writing, I become a better version of myself.

Writing is an expression of self, and I am worthy of being heard.

BIBLIOGRAPHY

The following is a list of books from which I pulled quotes and concepts for use in *Build Your Best Writing Life*. For more information on the topics discussed in this book, consider picking up the following resources:

~

Brown, Brené. *The Gifts of Imperfection: Let Go of Who You Think You're Supposed to Be and Embrace Who You Are.* Center City: Hazelden Publishing, 2010.

Bukowski, Charles. *Sunlight Here I Am: Interviews & Encounters, 1963–1993.* Northville: Sun Dog Press, 2003.

Bunting, Joe. "Ten Essential Quotes on Becoming a Writer (Plus One of My Own)," The Write Practice (blog), n.d., https://thewritepractice.com/becoming-a-writer-quotes/.

Cameron, Julia. *The Artist's Way: A Spiritual Path to Higher Creativity.* New York: Jeremy P. Tarcher/Putnam, 2002.

Canfield, Jack, with Janet Switzer. *The Success Principles: How to Get from Where You Are to Where You Want to Be*, 10th anniversary edition. New York: HarperCollins Publishers, 2015.

Chan, Yong Kang. *The Disbelief Habit: How to Use Doubt to Make Peace with Your Inner Critic.* N.p.: Author, 2017.

Clear, James. *Atomic Habits: An Easy and Proven Way to Build Good Habits and Break Bad Ones.* New York: Avery, 2018.

Foster, Lee. *An Author's Perspective on Independent Publishing: Why Self-Publishing May Be Your Best Option.* Berkeley: Foster Travel Publishing, 2016.

Friedman, Jane. *Publishing 101: A First-Time Author's Guide to Getting Published, Marketing and Promoting Your Book, and Building a Successful Career.* N.p.: Author, 2015.

Gaughran, Dave. *Let's Get Digital: How to Self-Publish, and Why You Should*, 3rd edition. N.p.: Author, 2018.

Gilbert, Elizabeth. *Big Magic: Creative Living Beyond Fear.* New York: Riverhead Books, 2015.

Goins, Jeff. *Real Artists Don't Starve: Timeless Strategies for Thriving in the New Creative Age.* New York: HarperCollins Leadership, 2017.

Grahl, Tim. *Your First 1000 Copies: The Step-by-Step Guide to Marketing Your Book.* Lynchburg: Out:think Group, 2013.

King, Stephen. *On Writing: A Memoir of the Craft.* New York: Pocket Books, 2000.

Lamott, Anne. *Bird by Bird: Some Instructions on Writing and Life*. New York: Random House, 2014.

Maraboli, Steve. *Life, the Truth, and Being Free*. N.p.: A Better Today Publishing, 2009.

Murakami, Haruki. *What I Talk About When I Talk About Running: A Memoir*. New York: Random House, 2008.

Penn, Joanna. *How to Make a Living with Your Writing: Books, Blogging and More*. N.p.: Curl Up Press, 2015.

Penn, Joanna. *Successful Self-Publishing: How to Self-Publish and Market Your Book*. N.p.: Curl Up Press, 2015.

Pressfield, Steven. *The War of Art: Break Through the Blocks and Win Your Inner Creative Battles*. New York: Black Irish Entertainment, 2011.

Rubin, Gretchen. *Better Than Before: Mastering the Habits of Our Everyday Lives*. New York: Random House, 2015.

Safford, David H. "'Writer's Block' Is a Lie—And It's Ruining Your Writing," The Write Practice (blog), n.d., https://thewritepractice.com/writers-block-lie/.

Tharp, Twyla. *The Creative Habit: Learn It and Use It for Life*, Reprint edition. New York: Simon & Schuster, 2003.

Thoreau, Henry David. *Walden and Civil Disobedience*, Reissue edition. New York: Signet, 2012.

ENDNOTES

2. Cultivating Confidence in Your Writing

1. https://www.bloomberg.com/news/videos/2015-10-15/oprah-winfrey-passion-is-energy

ABOUT THE AUTHOR

Kristen Kieffer is a fantasy fiction writer and the founder of Well-Storied.com, a website dedicated to helping writers craft sensational novels and build their best writing lives. Her website is frequently voted among the top sites for writers. When not putting pen to paper, Kristen can be found stargazing, wanderlusting, and playing with her rescue dog, Aggie.

instagram.com/kristen_kieffer

pinterest.com/well_storied

Made in the USA
Las Vegas, NV
13 January 2022

41272144R00125